of the Week
Activities & Projects for Building Literacy Skills

BOOK 2

Table of Contents

About This Book

Letter of the Week is a collection of 26 units, one for each letter of the alphabet. Each unit contains an art project, a reproducible activity, a creative-writing page, a literature extension idea, a recipe, a song or poem, and more!

How to Use This Book

Alphabet Book Pages

Each unit contains a reproducible book page for students to complete with their own art and dictated or written story ideas. Save each child's completed pages and compile them into a personalized alphabet book. A reproducible book cover is included on page 187 to add a finishing touch to each child's book. If you do not wish to make alphabet books, use each alphabet book page as a letter review/creative-writing activity sheet.

Award Certificate: Page 186

Reproduce the award on white or colored paper, providing one for each child. Fill in the blank spaces; then embellish the award with stickers if desired. Staple each child's award to the end of his completed alphabet book.

Alphabet Book Cover: Page 187

Reproduce page 187 on construction paper, providing one for each child. Encourage each child to decorate the cover with sponge-printed letters, stamped letters, letter stickers, or original drawings. Use the completed page as a book cover for each child's personal alphabet book.

Alphabet Character Clip Art: Pages 188–192

These pages contain ready-to-use clip art for all of the alphabet characters used in this book. Reproduce the characters as desired for the following possible uses:

Enlarge the patterns
- for shape booklet or journal covers
- for bulletin board characters

Reduce the patterns
- to embellish take-home notes or newsletters
- to glue onto flash cards
- to glue onto construction paper bookmarks

Use the patterns as shown for
- student awards
- nametags
- counting activities
- letter-to-picture matching activities

Bennington

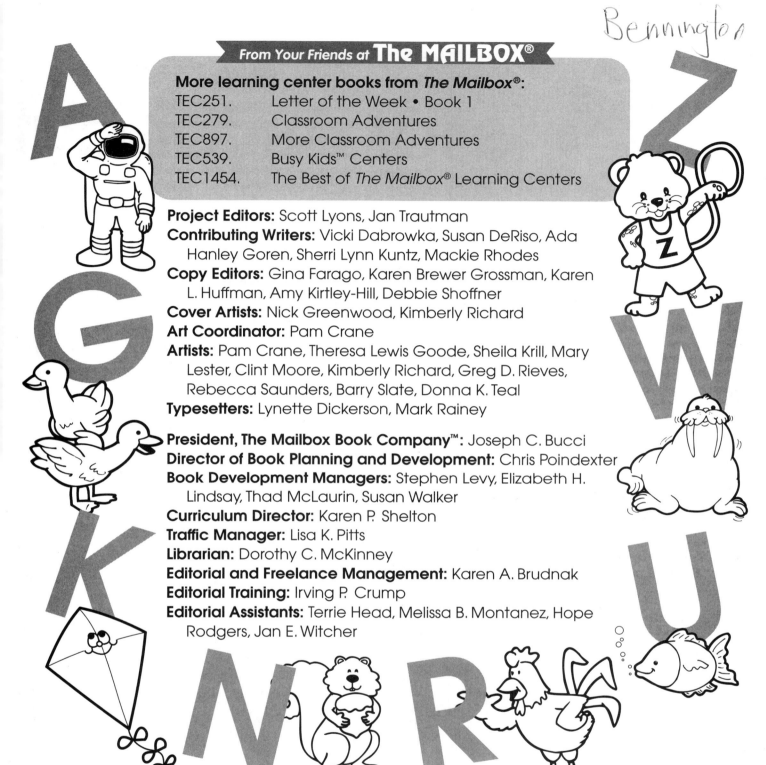

From Your Friends at **The MAILBOX®**

More learning center books from *The Mailbox*®:

Project Editors: Scott Lyons, Jan Trautman
Contributing Writers: Vicki Dabrowka, Susan DeRiso, Ada Hanley Goren, Sherri Lynn Kuntz, Mackie Rhodes
Copy Editors: Gina Farago, Karen Brewer Grossman, Karen L. Huffman, Amy Kirtley-Hill, Debbie Shoffner
Cover Artists: Nick Greenwood, Kimberly Richard
Art Coordinator: Pam Crane
Artists: Pam Crane, Theresa Lewis Goode, Sheila Krill, Mary Lester, Clint Moore, Kimberly Richard, Greg D. Rieves, Rebecca Saunders, Barry Slate, Donna K. Teal
Typesetters: Lynette Dickerson, Mark Rainey

President, The Mailbox Book Company™: Joseph C. Bucci
Director of Book Planning and Development: Chris Poindexter
Book Development Managers: Stephen Levy, Elizabeth H. Lindsay, Thad McLaurin, Susan Walker
Curriculum Director: Karen P. Shelton
Traffic Manager: Lisa K. Pitts
Librarian: Dorothy C. McKinney
Editorial and Freelance Management: Karen A. Brudnak
Editorial Training: Irving P. Crump
Editorial Assistants: Terrie Head, Melissa B. Montanez, Hope Rodgers, Jan E. Witcher

www.themailbox.com

Manufactured in the United States

10 9 8 7 6 5 4 3 2 1

A Is for Astronaut

Blast off your study of the letter A with these astronaut adventures designed for Grade A learning opportunities!

I'm a Little Astronaut

Your little ones will have great fun reading/ reciting and acting out this poem. In advance, write the poem on chart paper. After children are familiar with the poem, choose a child to highlight the *A*s in the first line of the poem. Choose a different child to do the same for each additional line of the poem.

I'm a little astronaut.
I climb into my suit.
I put on my helmet;
Then I give a big salute.
Ready for the countdown,
Saying ten, nine, eight.
I'm heading for the moon.
Oh, I can hardly wait!
Now I'm a little astronaut
Walking on the moon.
But please don't worry
'Cause I'll be home soon!

Action Astronaut

These astronauts take off with *A* words! In advance, collect a class supply of paper towel tubes. For each child, reproduce the rocket on page 6 and the *A* pictures on page 7. To begin, have each child color the rocket and then draw a picture of himself in the window at the top. Next, ask him to cut out the rocket and the pictures. Have him glue *only* pictures of things that begin with *A* to the rocket. Then have the child cover a paper towel tube with aluminum foil. Staple his completed rocket to the tube. Next, have the child tape strips of red, yellow, and orange tissue paper in the bottom of the tube. Ready for *A* action!

Astronaut Book Page

Use the *A* book page on page 8 as an individual worksheet. Have each child trace or write each letter in the space provided.

Then have her write or dictate to complete the story starter. If desired, instruct each child to save her page to use later after all the letters have been studied. Then have her use it with her other book pages to compile her own alphabet book.

Astronaut, Astronaut

In this fill-in-the-blank rhyme, your youngsters will get abundant practice in oral language! In advance, make an *A* cube by fitting together the bottom four inches of two half-gallon milk cartons. Cover the cube with construction paper or an adhesive covering. Duplicate page 9; then color and cut out the pictures. Glue a different picture to each side of the cube. Have your children chant the rhyme below, patterned after the text of Bill Martin's *Brown Bear, Brown Bear, What Do You See?* As you get to the blank, pass the cube to a child and ask him to roll it and then fill in the blank with the name of the picture that lands on the top. Repeat the activity until each child has had a turn to roll an *A* word.

Astronaut, Astronaut, what do you see?
I see an [*A word on cube*] looking at me!

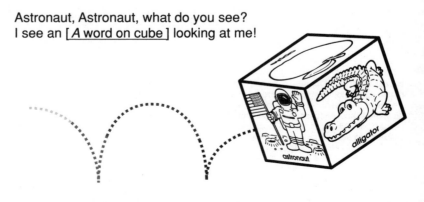

Blast Off! Poems About Space

Selected by Lee Bennett Hopkins

- "When I'm an Astronaut" by Bobbi Katz is a wonderful work of poetry for reinforcing astronaut vocabulary *and* launching dramatic play! Encourage each child to pretend she is an astronaut. Then read the poem aloud in echo fashion: you read one line and then students say it back to you. As they repeat each line back to you, encourage youngsters to get into the drama of it all! Ready for blastoff?

- What does the letter *A* have to do with walking on the moon? Well, here's a little astronaut trivia to offer your students. The first two men to walk on the moon were Neil *Armstrong* and "Buzz" *Aldrin*. Notice anything? After children discover that each man's last name begins with *A,* read aloud "First Moon Landing" by J. Patrick Lewis.

Astronaut Pudding

Once your little astronauts have blasted into space, they're sure to need a little nourishment! Prepare enough instant pudding for your whole class. For each child, scoop some pudding into a separate resealable plastic bag. Seal the bags; then pass them out. When everyone is ready to eat, snip off one bottom corner of each bag to make it a squeezable astronaut treat!

Astronaut Adventure

Sharpen memories with this listening and remembering game. In advance, duplicate the astronaut patterns (page 10) on construction paper. Color, cut out, and laminate the patterns. Glue the two astronauts together, back to back, sandwiching a large craft stick between the two cutouts. To play the game, seat children in a circle. Hold the astronaut puppet and say, "I'm an astronaut, and I'm going on an adventure. I'm taking a [insert a word]." Then pass the astronaut to the next child. Have her say, "I'm an astronaut, and I'm going on an adventure. I'm taking a…" Ask her to repeat what has already been mentioned and then add an idea of her own. Continue around the circle in the same manner until each child has had a turn.

Alice and Albert

Alice and Albert Astronaut are collectors. And what do they collect? *A* words, of course! Duplicate the astronauts on page 10. Label one cutout "Alice" and the other "Albert." Then color and cut out the astronauts. Glue each astronaut to a different top corner of a sheet of chart paper. During your *A* studies, encourage children to search for words that begin with *A*. Have them write new *A* words on the chart, color *A* pictures, or cut out and glue on pictures whose names begin with *A*. That's an "a-mazing" collection!

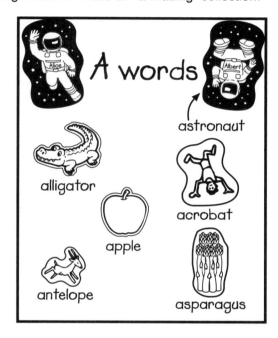

Literature Links

The Fantastic Cutaway Book of Spacecraft by Nigel Hawkes
Here in Space by David Milgrim
I Am an Astronaut by Cynthia Benjamin
I Want to Be an Astronaut by Byron Barton
Zoom! Zoom! Zoom! I'm Off to the Moon! by Dan Yaccarino

More Astronaut and *A* Activities

- Make an astronaut pointer by duplicating an astronaut pattern (page 7) on construction paper. (If desired, make one girl astronaut and one boy astronaut.) Color, cut out, and laminate the pattern. Then use a reusable adhesive to attach the astronaut to the end of a ruler or wooden dowel. Use the pointer to track text when reading aloud or for read-the-room activities.

- Youngsters read and remember *A* words with this version of the game Memory! Duplicate the *A* pictures on page 9 twice. Color, cut out, and laminate the pictures. Then place them in a center and have your students use them to play a game of Memory.

Rocket Pattern

Use with "Action Astronaut" on page 4.

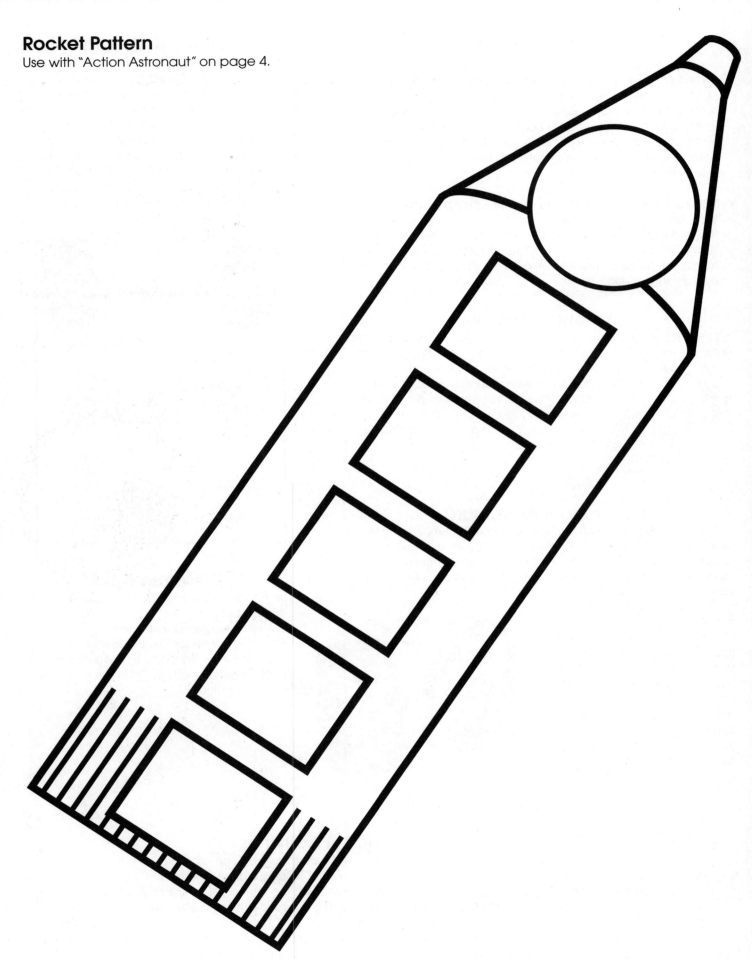

Astronaut Patterns
Use with "More Astronaut and *A* Activities" on page 5.

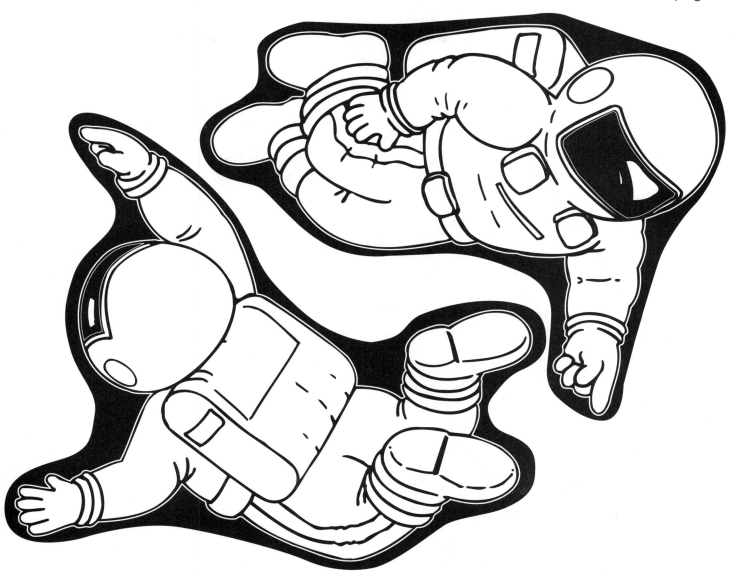

A   a

astronaut

This is me.

I am an astronaut!

I see…

Use with "Astronaut, Astronaut" on page 4 and "More Astronaut and *A* Activities" on page 5.

apple

alligator

anchor

astronaut

alphabet

ax

Astronaut Patterns

Use with "Astronaut Adventure" and "Alice and Albert" on page 5.

B Is for Boat

The sails are set for the letter B, *so everybody come aboard!*

Boat Book Page
Use the *B* book page on page 13 as directed for the letter *A*. Then have the child color the picture, adding details as desired. To finish the page, have her write or dictate to complete the story starter.

The Sails on the Boat
(sung to the tune of "The Wheels on the Bus")

The [sails] on the boat [go whoosh, whoosh, whoosh]!
[Whoosh, whoosh, whoosh]!
[Whoosh, whoosh, whoosh]!
The [sails] on the boat [go whoosh, whoosh, whoosh]
All across the sea.

Repeat the song using the words below to replace the underlined words in the first verse.

motor...goes vroom, vroom, vroom!
oars...go splash, splash, splash!
whistle...goes toot, toot, toot!
steering wheel...goes turn, turn, turn!
fisherman...says, "Come on, fish!"

Whoosh, whoosh, whoosh!

Bears in a Boat
Try this taste-tempting variation on an old standard. To prepare, duplicate the sails on page 14 on construction paper to make a class supply. Have each child color his sail and then glue it to the top of a craft stick. Next, instruct each child to fill the middle of a four-inch celery stick with peanut butter. Then have him poke the craft stick into the celery stick. Finally, nestle a few Teddy Grahams® inside the boat. There you have it—bears bobbing by in a boat!

Boat Builders
Duplicate the boat pattern on page 15 on construction paper to make a class supply. Have each child cut out his boat along the solid bold outline. Then instruct him to fold the boat along the dotted line. Have each child write his name on one side of his boat. Then invite each child to use art supplies to decorate the boat's other side. Help each child staple his boat along the side edges as shown. Use these boats for "Beautiful Boats" on page 12.

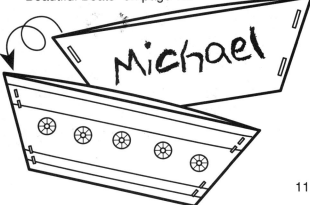

Michael

Beautiful Boats

Duplicate a set of the *B* pictures on page 16 for each child. Have each child color and cut apart the pictures. Then encourage children to manipulate their boats (made in "Boat Builders") and their *B* pictures according to the poem below.

Beautiful Boats
Beautiful boats bobbing on the sea.
Let's fill our boats with things that start with *B*:
A butterfly, a bat, a bird, and a bear.
We could even put a bride in there!
Let's keep on going, and you will see
A boy playing baseball and a bumblebee.
Add a few building blocks
And a cozy little bed,
A big balloon and a loaf of bread.
There are so many things that we can see
In a boat filled with things that start with *B*!

Row Row Row Your Boat
By Iza Trapani

In this book, a well-known, simple song is transformed into a delightful little adventure! Before sharing the story, sing "Row, Row, Row Your Boat" together. Then, as you begin to read the story aloud, have your students sing the first line ("Row row row your boat") of each stanza as you track the words. Then *you* sing the solo part as you finish up each stanza!

Boat Bingo

Make a class supply of page 17 plus one extra. Give each child a page and instruct him to color and cut apart the pictures at the bottom of the page. Then have him randomly glue each picture to a different space on the page, including the sail. Cut apart the cards on the extra page to use as your calling cards. Give your students beans, buttons, or bear counters to use as markers. To play, have each child put a marker on each picture that you call. When a student has marked three squares in a row, he calls out "Boat Bingo!" Vary this game by instructing children to cover all four corners and the sail.

Boat Books

The Boat Alphabet Book by Jerry Pallotta
Ferryboat Ride! by Anne Rockwell
I Love Boats by Flora McDonnell
The Little Boat by Kathy Henderson
My Father's Boat by Sherry Garland
Sail Away by Donald Crews

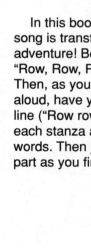

More Boat and *B* Activities

• Invite children to visit your block center and build boats out of blocks!

• Encourage youngsters to brainstorm a list of different types of boats. Let's see—there's a rowboat, a canoe, a motorboat, a kayak, a ship, a tugboat...My goodness, there's a bounty of boats!

B   b

boat

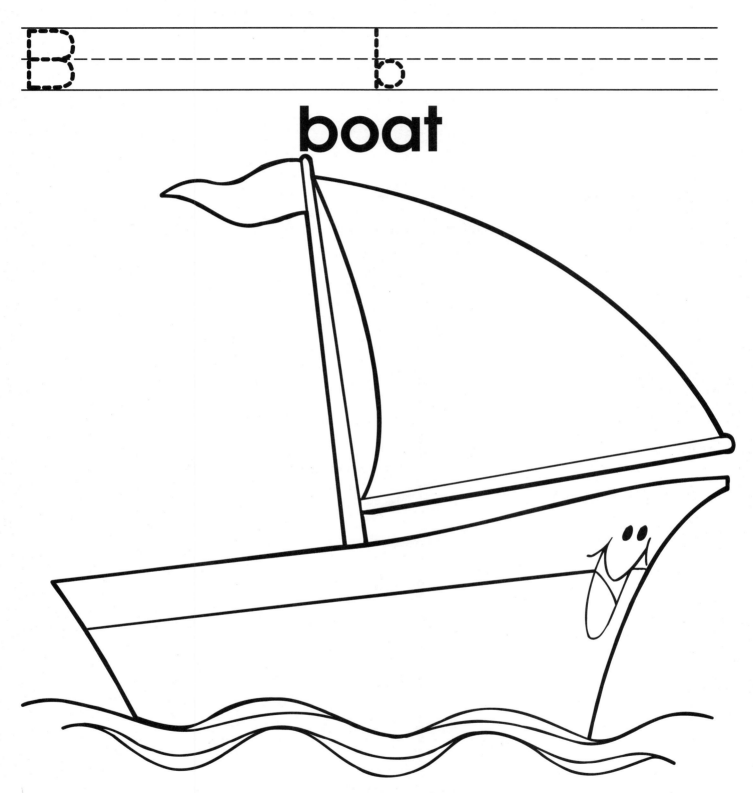

My boat bobbed on the water. I sailed to...

Sail Patterns
Use with "Bears in a Boat" on page 11.

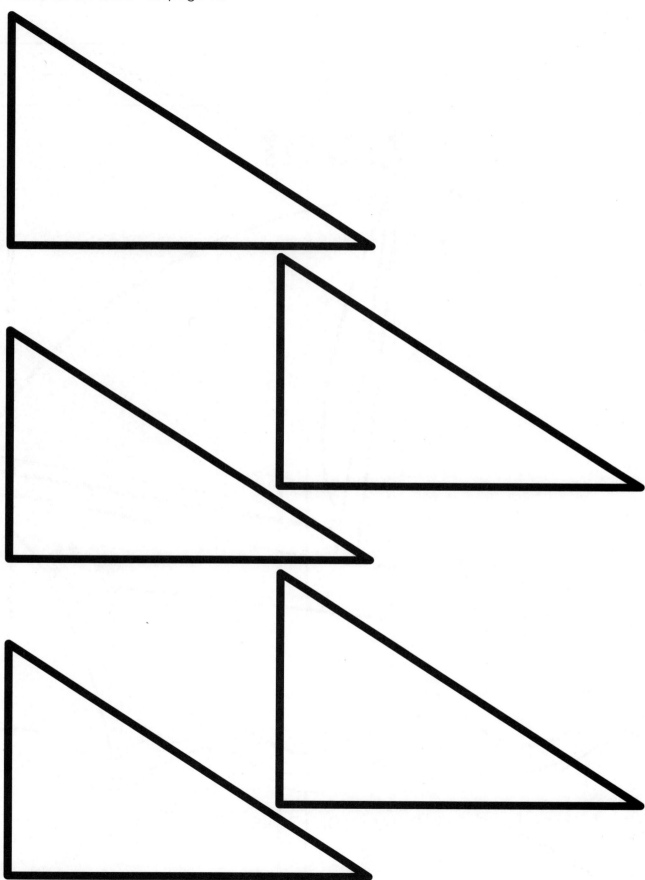

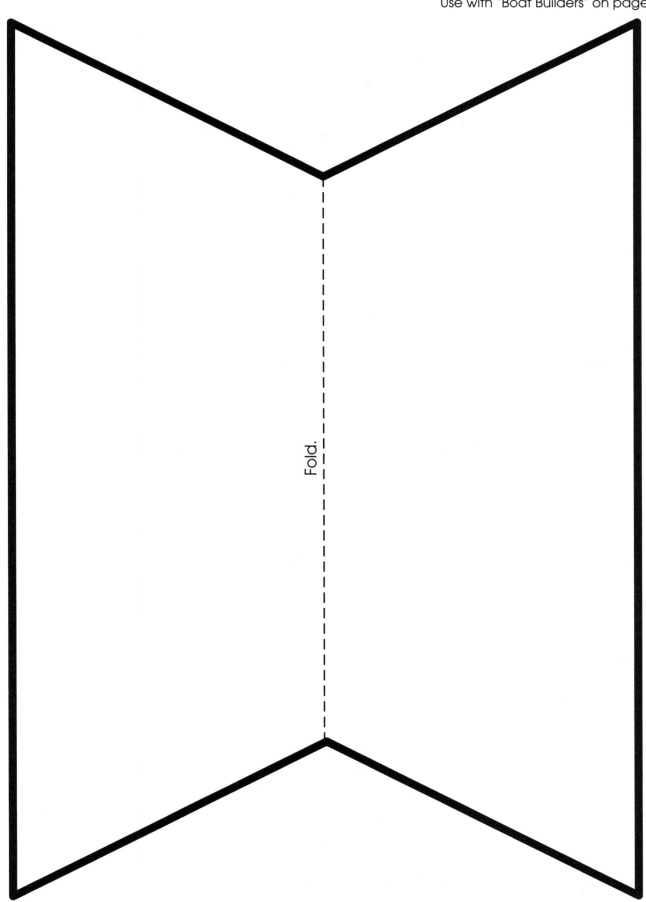

Fold.

B Pictures
Use with "Beautiful Boats" on page 12.

©2001 The Education Center, Inc. • *Letter of the Week—Book 2* • TEC603

Boat Bingo

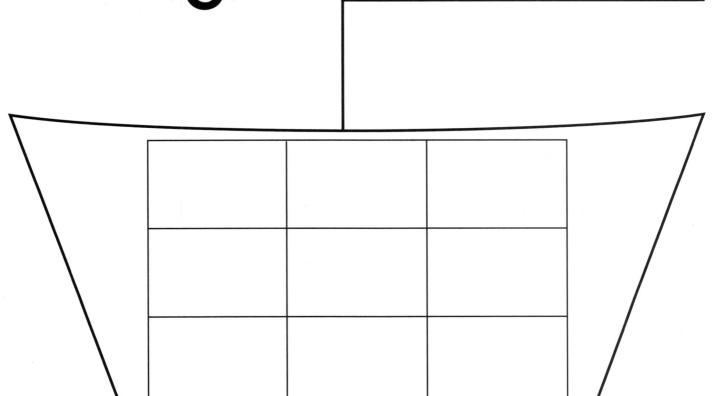

C Is for Cow

Calling all cows to the classroom to help reinforce the letter C!

Five Cranky Cows

Your kids will get a kick out of this little poem about—of all things—cranky cows! In advance, photocopy the cow pattern on page 22 on construction paper five times. Fold the construction paper so that you cut out each cow from a double thickness of paper. Glue each pair of cows together, inserting a wide craft stick handle between the two layers. Color (or have children color) one side of each cow puppet with a sad face. Color the other side of each cow with a happy face. Invite children to manipulate the cows according to the poem.

Five Cranky Cows

One cranky cow said,
"Moo, moo, moo!"
She found a friend;
Then there were two.

Two cranky cows
Swished their tails at a bee.
They found a friend;
Then there were three.

Three cranky cows
Went looking for one more.
They found a friend;
Then there were four.

Four cranky cows
Began to look alive.
They found a friend;
Then there were five.

When five cranky cows
Began to hang around,
Soon there were *zero*
Cranky cows to be found!

(Turn all cows around to show happy faces.)

Classroom Publishing

Use the poem "Five Cranky Cows" for the text of a child-illustrated class book. Begin by writing every two lines on a separate large sheet of construction paper. Then ask a different child or group of children to illustrate each page. Bind all the pages between two decorated covers; then invite each child to share his page with the class.

The Farmer and His Cow

(sung to the tune of "The Farmer in the Dell")

The farmer and his cow,
The farmer and his cow,
Moo, moo, the whole day through,
The farmer and his cow.

The farmer feeds his cow…
The farmer milks his cow…
The farmer walks his cow…
The farmer grooms his cow…
The farmer hugs his cow…

Clover the Crazy Cow Book Page

Use the *C* book page on page 20 as directed for the letter *A*. Have each child write or dictate to complete the story starter and then illustrate the page. *When Cows Come Home* by David L. Harrison is a great literature choice to get your youngsters' crazy cow thoughts in motion!

Cookie Cows

C is for cookie *and* cow, so here's a cooking project featuring both! Spread a little chocolate frosting on one end of a round sugar cookie. Add a dollop of whipped topping to the top to resemble a tuft of hair. Arrange almond wedges for horns, almond slivers for ears, and two small raisins for eyes. Use two sunflower seeds to resemble the cow's nose and one red string licorice to resemble its mouth. "Moo-velous!"

Clara's Cans

Clara the cow collects cans. But only very special cans belong in her collection—those that have pictures of *C* words! Reproduce page 21 and the pictures on page 22 for each child. Ask each child to color her pages and then cut out the pictures. Instruct her to glue only the pictures whose names begin with *C* in Clara's collection. Is the collection complete?

Collecting Cows

Share *Queen Nadine* by Maryann Kovalski with your class. After discussing this story about a cow and her special collection, extend the story with this collectible cow idea. In advance, duplicate the cow patterns on page 23 on white construction paper. Also make a copy of page 24 for each child. To begin, have each child color and cut out his patterns and then glue the pieces to a paper lunch bag. Then give each child two wiggle eyes to glue onto his cow. Have each child cut out his booklet pages and stack them together with the title page on top. Help each child staple his booklet along the left edge. Have each child store his booklet in his cow bag. Then instruct each child to search through old magazines to find and cut out *C* pictures. Instruct him to glue one *C* picture to each page of his booklet, adding more pages if needed. Then herd all the cows together on a tabletop. During small-group time, have each child share his booklet with the group.

My
C
Collection

by Shane

Car

Books for Your Cow Collection

Counting Cows by Woody Jackson
Cow by Jules Older
The New Baby Calf by Edith Newlin Chase
No Milk! by Jennifer A. Ericsson
Two Cool Cows by Toby Speed

More Cow and C Activities

- Encourage your students to brainstorm a list of foods made from milk. Then chant the sentence below together. Each time you get to the blank, ask a different child to complete the sentence. How long can you keep it going?

  Cows make milk, and milk makes [cheese].

- Of all the words that begin with *C,* perhaps *cookie* is still the all-time favorite. Cut and bake a slice of prepackaged cookie dough for each child in your class. Then invite each child to use cake decorations to top his cookie with a big letter *C!*

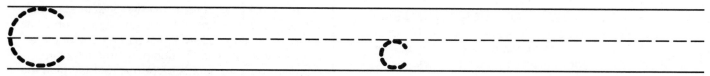

COW

Clover is a crazy cow.

She likes to...

Clara's Cans

Cow Pattern

Use with "Five Cranky Cows" on page 18.

C Pictures

Use with "Clara's Cans" on page 19.

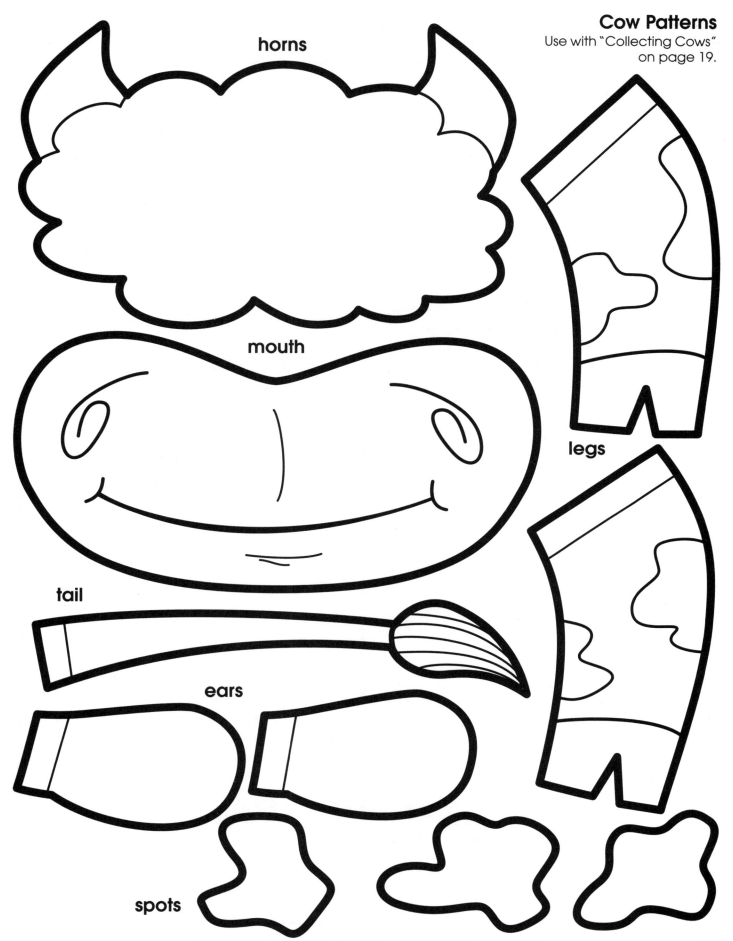

horns

mouth

legs

tail

ears

spots

My C Collection

by _____

©2001 The Education Center, Inc.

_____

_____

_____

D Is for Dog

Try these dandy dog activities to reinforce the letter D!

Dog Book Page

Use the *D* book page on page 27 as directed for the letter *A*. Invite each child to color the dog and design an award or treat for her canine companion. Then have each child write or dictate to complete the story starter.

Dog Decorations

These little pups will pep up any classroom!

Materials for each child:
half of a thin, white paper plate
two 6" x 3" construction paper rectangles (for the ears)
two 3" x 2" construction paper rectangles (for the paws)
3 black 2" construction paper squares (for the eyes and nose)
1 red 2" construction paper square (for the tongue)

Materials to share:

construction paper scraps	scissors
paintbrushes	glue
tempera paint (in dog colors)	markers

Give each child half of a paper plate and ask him to paint one side of it and then let the paint dry. Instruct him to position his plate with the straight edge at the top of his workspace (this is the dog's face). Then encourage him to cut out construction paper dog ears and paws. Have him glue those cutouts on the dog. Next, he cuts out two black eyes, a black nose, and a little red tongue to also glue onto the dog. Finally, he cuts out a bone, ribbon, toy, or ball from the construction paper scraps and glues it to his dog's paws. If desired, have him write a made-up dog's name on that cutout. Border a wall or door with these adorable dogs.

Everybody Has a Little Dog!

Customize an old childhood favorite, and you'll have a terrific vocabulary-building song. If desired, have children refer to the dogs they've made (see "Dog Decorations") to inspire ideas to fill in the blanks.

(sung to the tune of "Mary Had a Little Lamb")

[Casey] had a little dog, little
  dog, little dog.
[Casey] had a little dog; [his/
  her] fur was [spotted all
  over].
And everywhere that
  [Casey] went, [Casey]
  went, [Casey] went,
Everywhere that [Casey]
  went, the dog [jumped up
  and down].

Doggie Directions

Reinforce listening and following directions with this canine version of Simon Says. In advance, photocopy the dog bone (page 30) onto tagboard. Label one side of the bone with a male dog name beginning with *D* (such as Dexter Dog) and the other side with a female one (such as Daisy Dog). Punch a hole where indicated in the pattern and attach a length of yarn to make a necklace.

To play the game, the chosen leader (let's start with you) wears the dog-bone necklace with the appropriate male or female name showing. Play the game in the same manner as Simon Says, but say "Daisy Dog says" instead. Direct players to sit, speak, bark, lie down, roll over, chase their tails, shake, and so on.

In the Doghouse

What's in *this* doghouse? Anything whose name starts with the letter *D!* For each child, photocopy the doghouse (page 28) and make one or more copies of the doghouse doors (page 29). Have each child color her doghouse and color and cut out her doghouse doors. Instruct her to find and cut out magazine pictures of things whose names start with *D* (or work with a copy of the pictures on page 30). Have her glue each *D* picture onto a different doghouse door and label the picture. Then stack each child's doghouse doors and staple them to her doghouse. Encourage children to take their doghouses home and read the words to their families.

Dottie 's Doghouse

drum

Peanut Butter Pups

These Nutter Butter® cookie pups are quite popular! To make one, use peanut butter to "glue" on two almond slices for ears, two mini chocolate chips for eyes, and one M&M's minis® candy for a nose. Then use cake-decorating gel to draw a mouth. A perfect pup!

Shaggy, Waggy Dogs and Others

By Stephanie Calmenson

Share a book that brings each child along on a very special dog walk! After discussing the book, use the chant below to get your students spelling and cheering for dogs!

D-O-G-S
D-O-G-S— (Spell out the word.)
Dogs make really wonderful pets!
They like to play. They like to run.
Give them love and have some fun!
D-O-G-S—
Dogs make really wonderful pets!

Yea, dogs!

Dog Books

The Adventures of Taxi Dog by Debra and Sal Barracca
Bark, George by Jules Feiffer
The Bookshop Dog by Cynthia Rylant
The Five-Dog Night by Eileen Christelow
Little Dog Poems by Kristine O'Connell George
McDuff Moves In by Rosemary Wells
Ten Silly Dogs: A Countdown Story by Lisa Flather
Why Benny Barks by David Milgrim

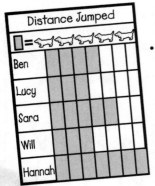

Distance Jumped

Ben							
Lucy							
Sara							
Will							
Hannah							

More Dog and *D* Activities

- Use these dogs to help reinforce measuring skills. Photocopy a supply of the dachshund patterns (page 31) on light brown construction paper. Cut apart the pictures and laminate them. Divide students into groups of three. Have one child stand at a masking tape line, pretend to be a dog, and then jump as far as he can. Instruct the other two children to use the dog pictures to measure the distance. Have them record the distance. Then repeat the process for the other two members of the group. Later, make a class graph for each small group's results. And the greatest doggie distance is…?

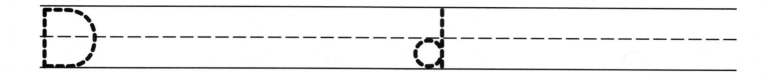

dog

This darling dog wins first place with me because...

_____'s

Doghouse

Dd

Pictures

Use with "In the Doghouse" on page 26.

Dog Bone Pattern

Use with "Doggie Directions" on page 25.

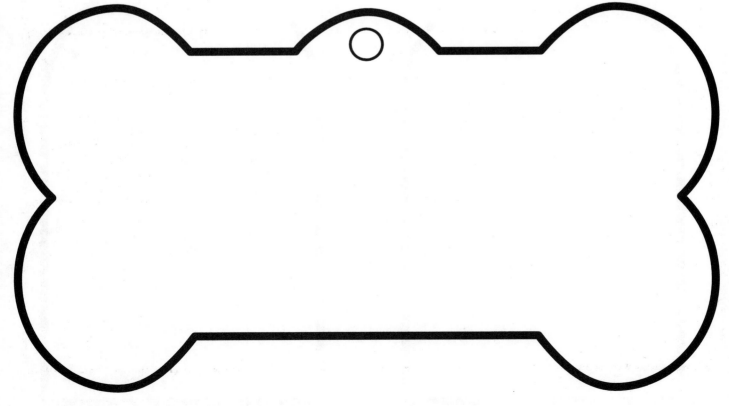

©2001 The Education Center, Inc. • *Letter of the Week—Book 2* • TEC603

E Is for Elf

Join these energetic elves for some letter E fun!

Busy Little Elves

All the little elves are busy doing their jobs! Entice your youngsters to explore careers with the rhyme below. First, collect objects or pictures related to a variety of jobs. Then ask a child to pick something from the collection. Have him name a worker who uses that item in his job. Next, recite the rhyme, using the name of the worker in the third line. During the second sentence in the third line, have the child model (or pantomime) how the object is used in the job. Then invite the whole class to imitate his actions. Conclude the rhyme with the last line. Repeat the activity to give each child a turn to pick an object and name a worker.

I'm a busy little elf and I'm here to say
That I do my job and I earn my pay.
I am a [painter]. I do my job this way.
And when my work is done, I head home for
  the day!

Elf Book Page

Use the *E* book page on page 34 as directed for the letter *A*. Exercise youngsters' imaginations with the energetic elf. Have each child write or dictate to complete the story starter. Then have him illustrate his ideas.

Elf Edibles

Little ones will be eager to sink their teeth into these tasty elf snacks. To begin, prepare two batches of instant vanilla pudding. Then mix green food coloring into one batch and blue food coloring into the other. Give each child a graham cracker and several Keebler® Elf Grahams®. To make a snack, the child spreads the two pudding colors onto her cracker to create green grass and a blue sky. Then she arranges her elves on the cracker to complete the scene. Excellent eats!

Elf Art

Invite students to enter into their own worlds of creativity to make these interesting elves. To prepare, provide a few large egg-shaped tagboard tracers in your art center along with large sheets of skin-toned construction paper and an assortment of craft items. Ask each child to trace and cut out an egg shape from her choice of skin-toned paper. Then invite her to use craft items to create her own original elf.

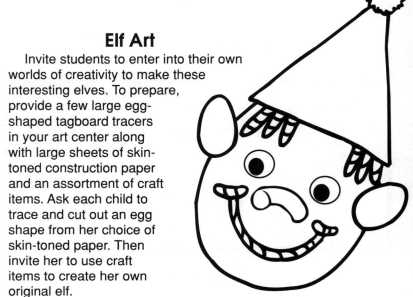

Elf Houses

Have you heard that elves live in hollowed-out trees? Well, these trees happen to be filled with *E*s! Give each child two copies of page 35 and one copy each of pages 36 and 37. Help each child label one elf house "short *E*" and the other elf house "long *E*." Have each child color the tree and the pictures on the doors. Then have him color one blank door on each page to look like the bark of the tree. Ask each child to cut out the pictures and sort them by short and long *E* sounds. Help each child stack and staple the doors and pictures to the corresponding trees. (The blank doors are for original *E* words that your children might discover!)

Elfabet: An ABC of Elves
By Jane Yolen

The exquisite illustrations in this book will easily inspire your elf-artists to create their own alliterative masterpieces. After sharing the book, help each child create an alliterative sentence about her "elf" self, loosely following the text pattern in the book. Write her dictation, which might refer to a real or an imaginary situation, at the bottom of a large sheet of paper. Then have the child print or stamp the corresponding letter at the top of her page. Ask her to illustrate her page to match the text. Then call students in "elf-abetical" order to share their pictures with the class.

Elf Tales

Child of Faerie, Child of Earth by Jane Yolen
The Elf's Hat by Brigitte Weninger
The Elves and the Shoemaker retold by
    Bernadette Watts
The Oldest Elf by James Stevenson
    (Christmas related)

More Elf and *E* Activities

• Reproduce the enter and exit signs (page 38) on construction paper. Color the elves; then cut out and laminate the signs. Post the large ones on your doors. (If you just have one door, post each sign on the right side of the door in the appropriate direction.) Invite your students to use the little signs in your block area. Encourage children to build a building or elf habitat and use the signs to mark the entrance and exit.

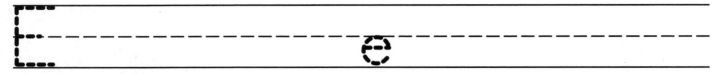

elf

This little elf has so much energy!

He likes to…

Elf House

E e

Door Patterns (short E)
Use with "Elf Houses" on page 33.

elephant

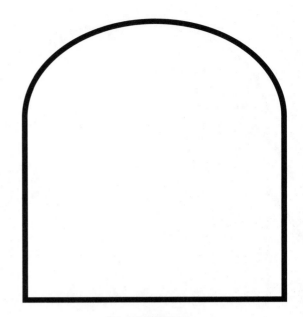

envelope

eggs

engineer

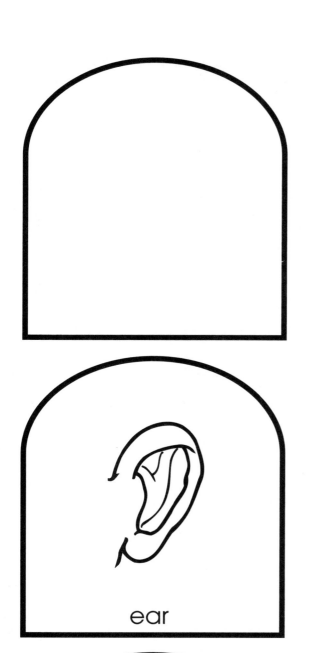

ear

eagle

easel

eel

Sign Patterns

Use with "More Elf and *E* Activities" on page 33.

©2001 The Education Center, Inc. • *Letter of the Week—Book 2* • TEC603

©2001 The Education Center, Inc. • *Letter of the Week—Book 2* • TEC603

©2001 The Education Center, Inc.   ©2001 The Education Center, Inc.

F Is for Fox

Use these frisky fox activities to reinforce the letter F.

Fox Book Page

Use the *F* book page on page 41 as directed for the letter *A.* Help each child read the text at the bottom of the page; then have him illustrate and write or dictate to complete the story starter.

Fox Faces

Fancy these fox faces popping up all over your classroom! In advance, make a class supply of the fox face pattern (page 44) on orange, red, or gray construction paper. For each fox, also provide one matching four-inch construction paper square, black and yellow construction paper scraps, a few lengths of raffia, and a black crayon. To begin, help each child cut out her fox face pattern and roll and staple it into a cone. Have her cut out two black eyes and one black nose. Instruct each child to glue raffia whiskers to the back of the nose. Then have her glue the eyes and the nose to the fox, adding yellow construction paper eye highlights. Next, show each child how to cut her square in half diagonally to make two ears. Have her color a black outline around each ear and then glue the ears onto her fox. Staple each fox to a bulletin board to create a forest full of 3-D foxes.

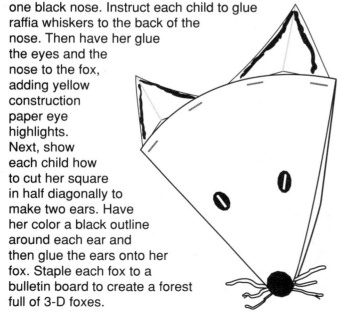

A Flower for Fox

Fox has a fancy flower—and it's full of words that begin with *F!* Reproduce page 42 and the petal patterns on page 43 for each child. Ask each child to color and cut out the flower petals that have pictures that begin with *F* on them. Then have him fold over each tab and glue it on the flower where indicated. Invite each child to complete his project by coloring the rest of the page. Pretty fancy flower, Fox!

Do a Little Fox-Trot

A familiar tune with just a few "fox-worthy" changes makes this the perfect song for your fox unit!

(sung to the tune of "The Hokey-Pokey")

You put your [front paw] in.
You put your [front paw] out.
You put your [front paw] in and you shake it (them) all about.
You do a little fox-trot and you turn yourself around.
That's what it's all about.

Repeat the song, replacing the underlined words with *back paw, fox ears, fluffy tail,* and *little nose.*

Hattie and the Fox
By Mem Fox

Hattie can tell that trouble—in the form of a fox—is lurking close by. And although she tries and tries to summon the attention of her friends, they respond with these questions: Who cares? So what? What next? Well, before long *everybody* cares—but is it too late? Before sharing this crowd pleaser with your youngsters, reproduce the animal patterns (pages 43 and 45) on construction paper. (If desired, enlarge the patterns first.) Color, cut out, and laminate each animal. Glue a craft stick to the back of each cutout to make stick puppets. After sharing the story, invite students to manipulate the puppets as you read the story again. As they are able, encourage children to take over more and more of the speaking parts.

Fox Recipe

This fox is the child-made edible kind! For each child you'll need one slice of bread, some pimento cheese spread, two black olives, a plastic knife, and a paper plate. Instruct a child to cut out a large triangle face and two triangle ears from his slice of bread. Have him arrange the face and ears and then spread the pimento cheese spread over them. Next, have him slice one olive in half and use those slices for eyes. The final touch is the whole olive nose.

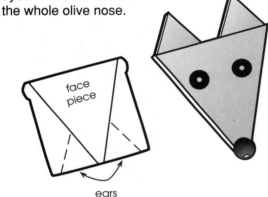

face piece

ears

More Fox Tales

City Foxes by Susan J. Tweit
Ice Bear and Little Fox by Jonathan London
Red Fox by Karen Wallace
Red Fox Running by Eve Bunting

More Fox and *F* Activities

- Can you *outfox* a fox? Little Flossie Finley does just that in *Flossie and the Fox* by Patricia C. McKissack. Before sharing this story, ask children what they think the term *outfox* means. Then read the story aloud. Ask students to tell you how Flossie outfoxed the fox; then write a class definition for the word. Afterward, encourage children to share this new vocabulary word with their families.

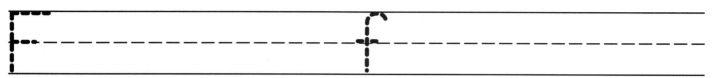

fox

This frisky fox has fun in the forest.

He...

Name _____

A Flower for Fox

Note to the teacher: Use with "A Flower for Fox" on page 39.

Petal Patterns
Use with "A Flower for Fox" on page 39.

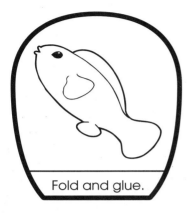

Fold and glue.

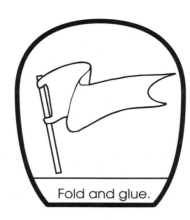

Fold and glue.

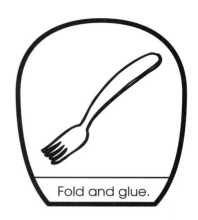

Fold and glue.

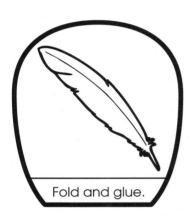

Fold and glue.

Fold and glue.

Fold and glue.

Animal Patterns
Use with *Hattie and the Fox* on page 40.

Fox Face Pattern
Use with "Fox Faces" on page 39.

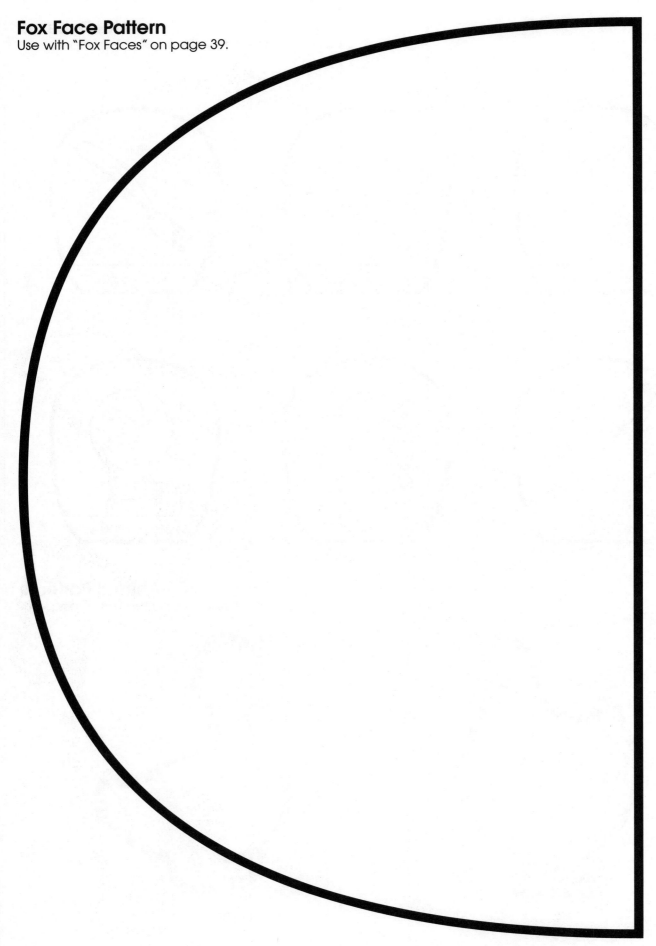

G Is for Goose

Grab up these great goose activities to teach children about geese and the letter G!

Goose Egg on the Loose!

Use this idea to practice letter recognition and phonics. In advance, collect a class supply of plastic eggs. Put a letter *G* inside one of the eggs. (It can be a magnet letter, written on a piece of paper, molded from clay, or anything else you can think of!) Seat children in a circle on the floor and give each child an egg. As you begin reciting the rhyme below, instruct the children to pass the eggs around the circle. When you say "three," have each child open the egg he is holding at that time. Whoever has the *G* gives his egg to you and the *G* to another child. Then he goes to the pond (the middle of the circle) to become a goose in the forming gaggle. The child who was given the *G* puts it in her egg. Begin the rhyme again and proceed in the same manner. But this time, in order to join the gaggle of geese in the pond, the person who has the *G* must say a *G* word. When she says a *G* word, members of the existing gaggle honk a welcome. Continue until each child has joined the gaggle of geese in the pond.

There is a goose egg on the loose!
Just who has it is hard to tell.
To find the egg that comes from a goose
We'll have to look inside the shell.
One…two…three!

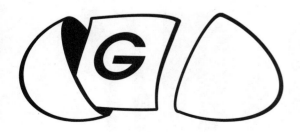

Goose's Gift Book Page

Use the *G* book page on page 48 as directed for the letter *A*. Have each child write or dictate to complete the story starter. Then have her color the page.

Honk! Honk! A Story of Migration
By Mick Manning and Brita Granström

Take a magical journey with a wild goose and her flock as they migrate north. This fact-based story makes learning fun! In advance, make a class supply of page 52. Then share the book with your class. Afterward, give each child a copy of page 52. Ask her to color and cut apart the pictures. Then have her glue them in sequence, from left to right, to show the sequence of the story. Honk! Honk!

Goose Eggs

These goose nests look good enough to eat—and they are! To make these sweet treats, melt one can of chocolate frosting over low heat. Stir in one large can of chow mein noodles. Let the mixture cool slightly; then give each child a lime-sized portion of the mixture and a sheet of waxed paper. Encourage her to shape the mixture into a nest and add five or six light-colored malted milk balls or jelly beans. (This recipe yields about ten nests.)

Note: Geese usually lay five to six eggs. They can be creamy white, blue, or greenish.

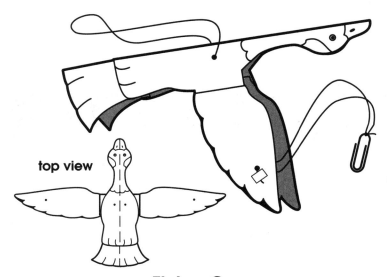

top view

Flying Geese
Children can actually flap the wings of these flying geese!

Materials for each child:
tagboard goose patterns (pages 49–50)
scissors
crayons
glue
hole puncher (to share)
two 36" lengths of string
paper clip
tape

In advance, copy the goose patterns onto tagboard to make a class supply. Have each child cut out his patterns. Demonstrate how to glue the tail feathers and wings onto the goose; then have each child assemble his own goose. Next, instruct each child to punch a hole in each wing where indicated. Then have him fold his goose along the dotted line and punch another hole (through both thicknesses of the body) where indicated. Have each child unfold and color his goose. For each goose, tie a paper clip to the center of a 36" length of string. Thread each end of that string through a different hole in the wings and then tape the ends to the wings. Thread the other length of string through the holes in the body and tie it to make a hanger. Hang the goose with the colored side facing the ceiling. To see the geese fly, have children gently pull on the paper clips.

More Goose Tales
Boo to a Goose by Mem Fox
Catching the Wind by Joanne Ryder
The Day the Goose Got Loose by Reeve Lindbergh
Duck, Duck, Goose? retold by Katya Arnold
Goose by Molly Bang
The Goose That Almost Got Cooked by Marc Simont
Just You and Me by Sam McBratney

Six Little Geese
This is a great little song for a lighthearted follow-up to a reading of *Honk! Honk! A Story of Migration* by Mick Manning and Brita Granström. Or just sing it for the thematic fun of it—not to mention great goose-counting practice!

Six Little Geese
(sung to the tune of "Six Little Ducks")

[Six] little geese that I once knew
Headed for the North and flew and flew.
But one little goose needed a rest
So he honked good-bye and flew back to the nest,
Back to the nest.
He honked good-bye and flew back to the nest.

Last Verse:
One little goose that I once knew
Headed for the North and flew and flew.
When he saw he was the only goose in the sky,
He honked to the others with a "bye, bye, bye!"
"Bye, bye, bye!"
He honked to the others with a "bye, bye, bye!"

Goose's Gaggle
A group of geese is called a *gaggle,* and this goose seems to have lost her gaggle! Give each child a copy of page 51. After introducing the word *gaggle,* read the directions together. Then have each child complete the page to help the goose find her gaggle.

More Goose and *G* Activities
- Play Duck, Duck, Goose!

- Share a collection of Mother Goose stories.

- During a designated time, encourage children to "fly" around the playground and honk like geese.

G g

goose

Goose has a gift.

I think it is a(n)...

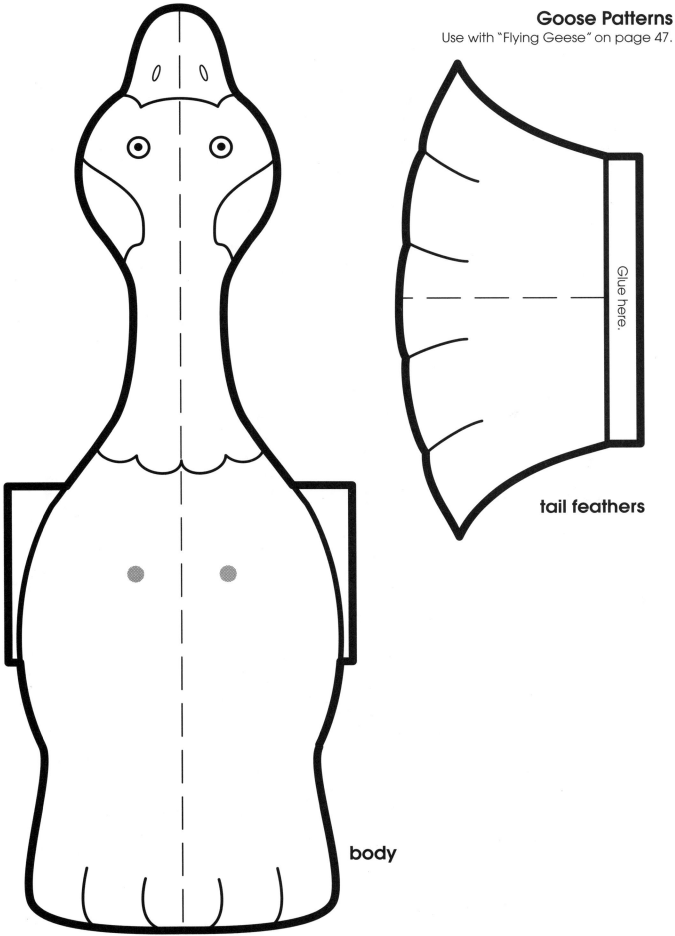

Glue here.

tail feathers

body

Goose Patterns
Use with "Flying Geese" on page 47.

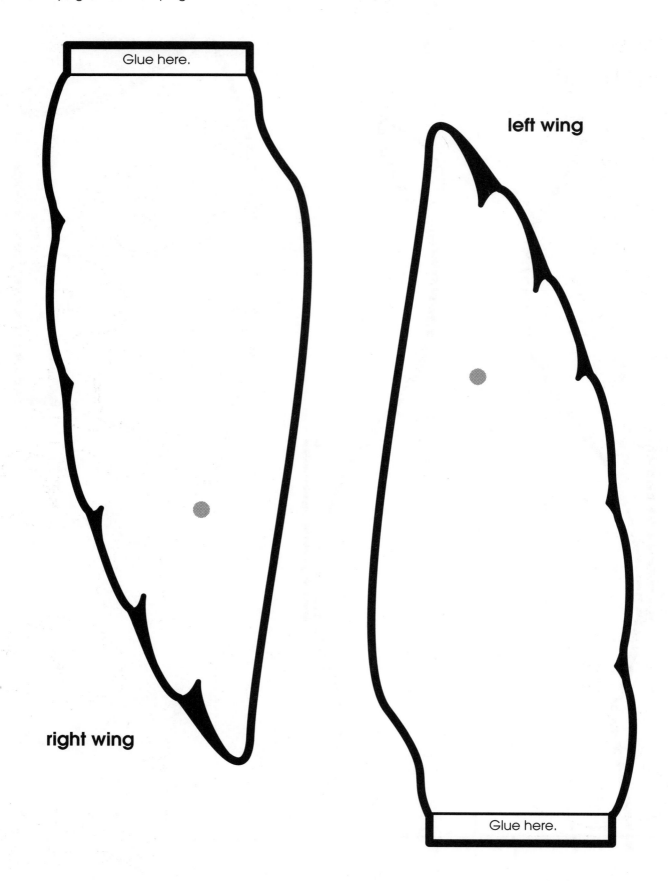

Glue here.

left wing

right wing

Glue here.

Goose's Gaggle

Goose has lost her gaggle!
Help her find her way.
Color all the clouds with a *g*.

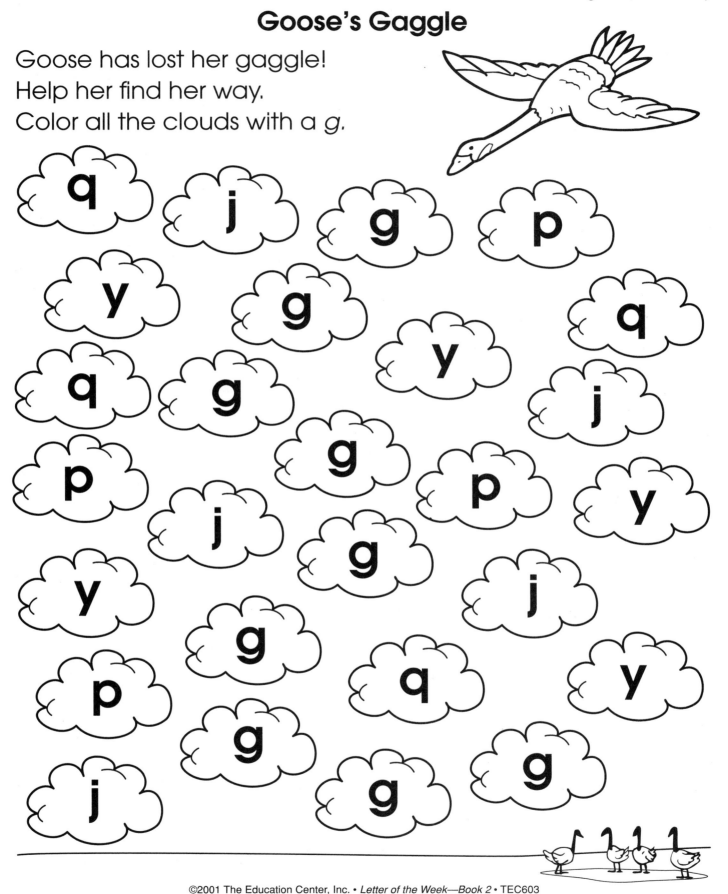

Name _____

Honk! Honk!

✂ Cut. ⬅ Glue.

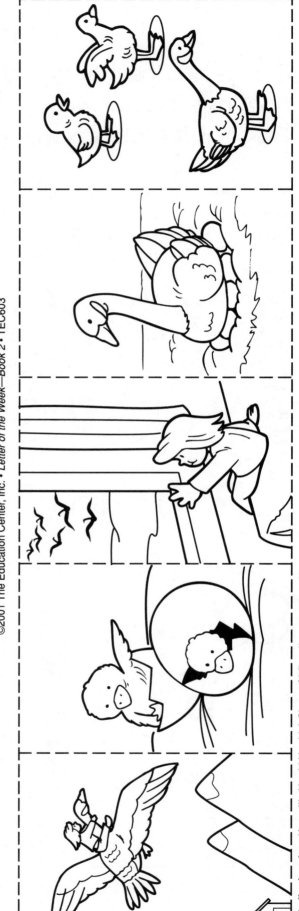

©2001 The Education Center, Inc. • *Letter of the Week—Book 2* • TEC603

Note to the teacher: Use with *Honk! Honk! A Story of Migration* on page 46.

H Is for House

Build a foundation for learning the letter H with these house activities.

House Fingerplay

Teach youngsters the accompanying hand motions for each line of this poem.

Some houses have windows and doors.
   (Trace square in the air.)
Some houses have ceilings and floors.
   (Point up, then down.)
Some houses are small,
   (Use hands to indicate small.)
And some have it all,
   (Sweep both hands upward in front of body, then to sides.)
But the best house, you know, is yours!
   (Point to "you.")

Tasty Toast House

Have little ones create these delicious dwellings for a snack they'll want to try again at home! To make one, spread peanut butter on a slice of toast. Add a single section of graham cracker for a door. Put a small dab of peanut butter on one side of an M&M's® candy; then stick it to the door to make a doorknob. Add bite-sized graham crackers to make windows and a chimney. Mmm...who's hungry for a house?

House Book Page

Use the *H* book page on page 55 as directed for the letter *A*. Have each child illustrate the page and write or dictate to complete the story starter.

Design a House

Duplicate the house patterns on page 56 and the door and window patterns on page 57 on white construction paper for each child. Invite each child to choose one of the house patterns to cut out and color as she desires. Then have her color and cut out the doors and windows of her choice and glue them to her house. For each child, roll one half of a sentence strip into a circle and staple the ends together. Then staple the child's finished house to the circle (as shown) so that the rolled sentence strip forms a stand. Display these stand-up houses on a tabletop to form a street scene or a whole neighborhood!

"I'm a Little House"

Sing this action song to the tune of "I'm a Little Teapot."

I'm a little house
So neat and small.
Here is my roof.
   (Touch fingertips together overhead.)
Here are my walls.
   (Bring hands straight down at sides.)
When you come to visit on my block,
   (Motion "come here.")
Just step to my door and knock, knock, knock!
   (Step forward; pretend to knock.)

Cut-and-Paste House

Duplicate the cut-and-paste house pattern (page 58) and the picture cards (page 57) on white construction paper for each child. Have each student color and cut out the pictures of things that begin with the letter *H*. Then have each child glue his *H* pictures to the windows on his house.

To make this activity a learning center, duplicate the house pattern and pictures onto sturdy tagboard. Color all the pieces, cut apart the pictures, and then laminate everything for durability. Store the house and loose picture cards in a large zippered plastic bag. To use the center, a child chooses the pictures that begin with the letter *H* and then places them on the windows of the house.

A House for Hermit Crab
By Eric Carle

Hermit Crab had a fine time decorating his new home—and your youngsters will, too! For each child, duplicate the large shell pattern on page 59 on white construction paper. Invite each of your little artists to use watercolor paints, construction paper, tissue paper, wallpaper samples, markers, crayons, or glitter glue to decorate the shell as he desires. Have each child write or dictate to complete the story starter. Then display the finished projects on a bulletin board.

Cassidy

A hermit crab would like this shell because...
it has lots of colors.

Hooray for House Books!

Building a House by Byron Barton
A House Is a House for Me by Mary Ann Hoberman
Houses and Homes by Ann Morris
The Little House by Virginia Lee Burton
My House by Lisa Desimini

More House and *H* Activities

- Bring in pages from the real estate section of your weekend newspaper. For each child, pencil a large letter *H* onto a sheet of paper. Then have each student cut out small house pictures from the paper and glue them over the penciled lines to form the letter *H*.

- Play a game of House Hopscotch. Cut ten simple house shapes from various colors of construction paper. Adhere the houses to the floor with clear Con-Tact® paper in a traditional hopscotch layout. Use a plastic house from a Monopoly® game instead of a pebble. Little ones will love hopping on houses!

- Hold a house hunt. Hide a number of small plastic houses (from a Monopoly® game) or laminated pictures of houses around your classroom. Divide your class into teams and challenge each team to find as many houses as possible in the allotted time. Provide a letter *H* reward to all the players, such as Honeycomb® cereal or Hershey's® Hugs® candy. Then put the houses in your block area for children to use as they build neighborhoods.

H h

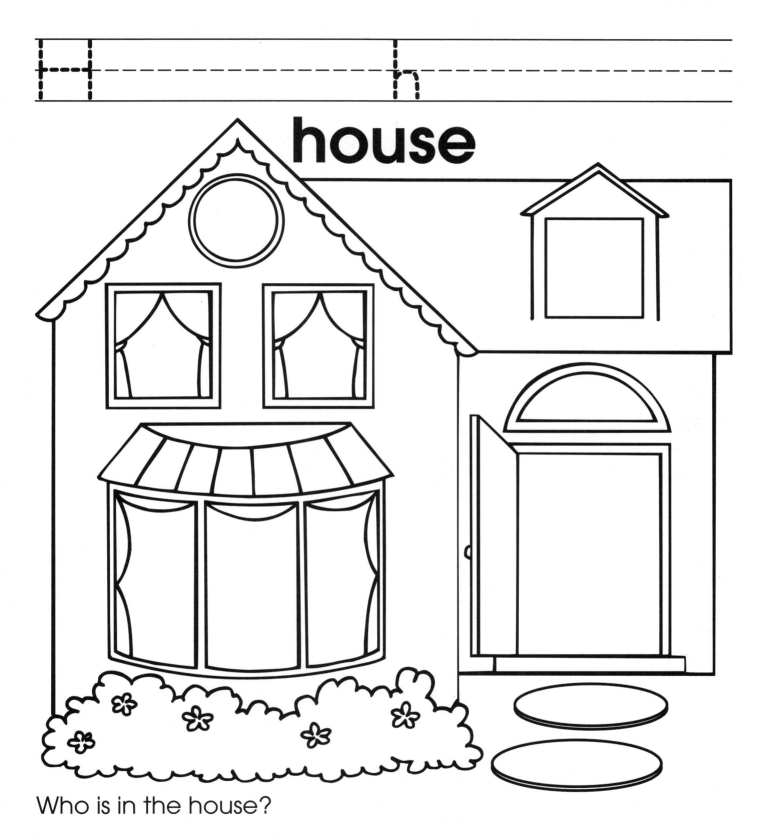

house

Who is in the house?

I see…

House Patterns
Use with "Design a House" on page 53.

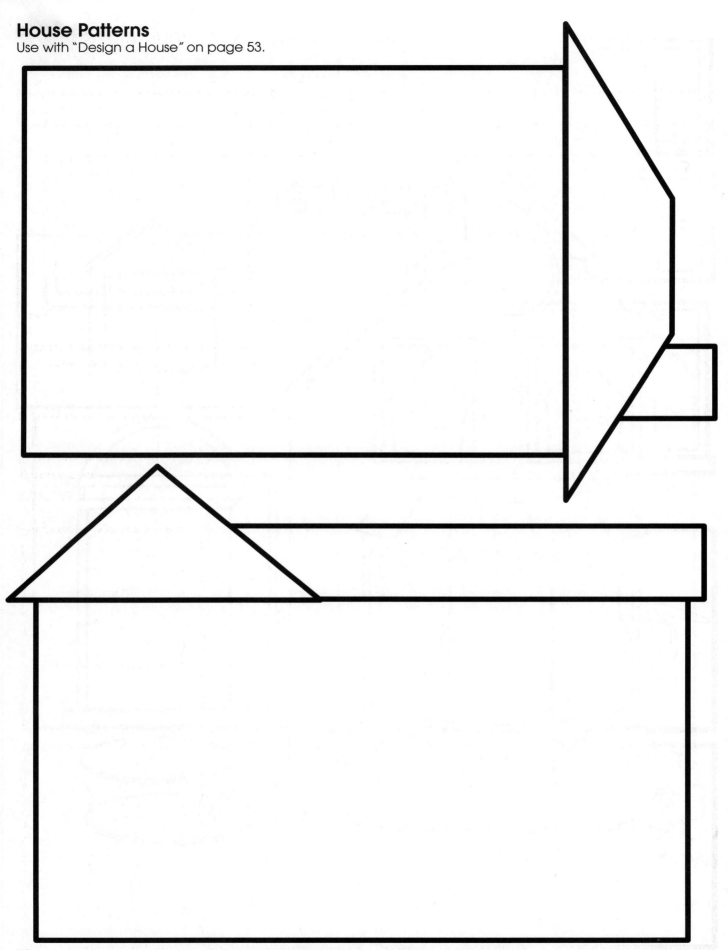

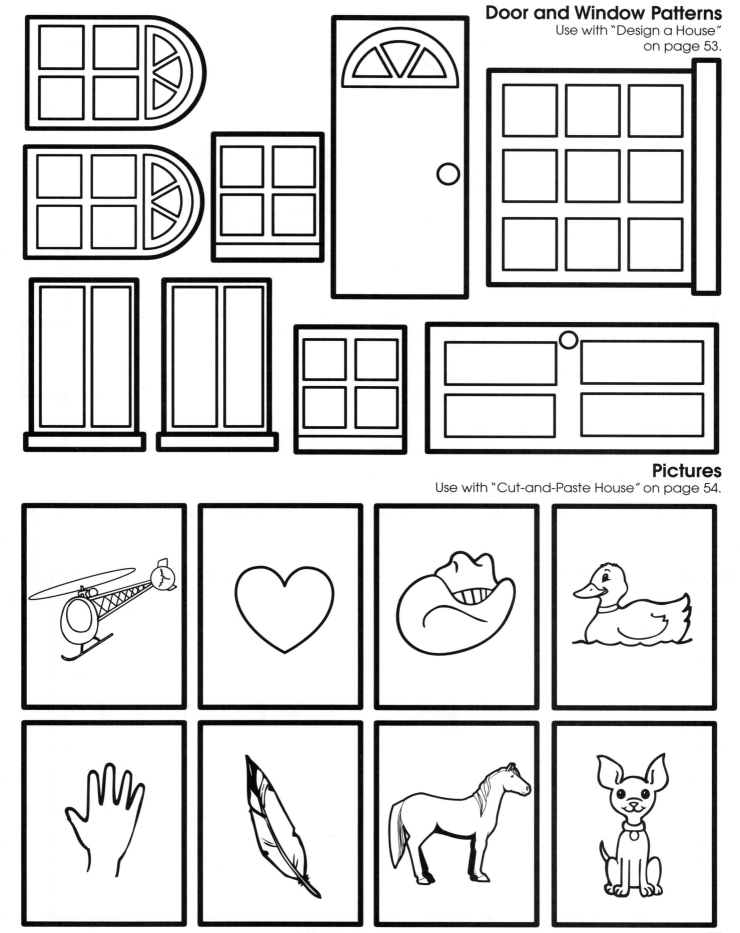

Door and Window Patterns
Use with "Design a House"
on page 53.

Pictures
Use with "Cut-and-Paste House" on page 54.

Cut-and-Paste House Pattern
Use with "Cut-and-Paste House" on page 54.

A hermit crab would like this shell because…

I Is for Inchworm

Creep into learning about the letter I with the help of a friendly little inchworm!

Five Little Inchworms

Before teaching little ones this poem, use washable markers to draw a green worm with two black dot eyes on each fingertip of one of your hands. There you go—five little inchworms!

Five little inchworms were creeping right along.

The first one said, "This is taking much too long!"

The second one said, "I'd rather stay and play!"

The third one said, "Let's just rest today!"

The fourth one said, "Oh no, we have to eat!"

And the fifth one said, "This leaf could be a treat!"

So they munched and they munched with a "munch, munch munch,"

And the five little inchworms had a very tasty lunch!

The Teeny-Tiny Inchworm

Invite your little ones to make up the motions as they sing this song to the tune of "The Itsy-Bitsy Spider."

The Teeny-Tiny Inchworm
The teeny-tiny inchworm
Went inching up a tree.
His journey took so long
As you can plainly see.
But he kept on inching
All through the day and night.
And the teeny-tiny inchworm
Went inching out of sight!

Inchworm Book Page

Use the *I* book page on page 62 as directed for the letter *A*. Have each child draw a picture of something for the inchworm to measure. Then have the child write or dictate to complete the story starter.

Artwork That Measures Up

Move your youngsters into measurement skills with this fun art project. To prepare, make several inchworm measuring sticks by hot-gluing a one-inch length of green pipe cleaner onto each of several craft sticks (as shown). Then give each child a sheet of white construction paper. Ask him to draw a picture of something tall. When he's finished drawing, instruct him to measure the height of his drawing by aligning the bottom of an inchworm (green pipe cleaner piece) with the bottom of his drawing and then using a pencil to mark a line at the top of the worm. Have him label the line with a number 1. Help him continue to measure and mark each inch until he reaches the top of his picture. (Round off to the closest inch.) Then write his dictation as he describes the height of his drawing.

Inchworm Nibblers

Here's an itty-bitty snack your young chefs can make all by themselves! To prepare, tint a container of white frosting green. Then set the container on a table along with a bowl of miniature chocolate chips and a bowl of pretzel sticks. Give each child a paper plate and a craft stick; then encourage her to make several inchworm nibblers. To make one, she holds one end of a pretzel stick while using her craft stick to spread green frosting over an inch (or more) of the other end. She presses on two mini chocolate chips for eyes. Then she's ready to inch that snack right up to her mouth and take a nibble!

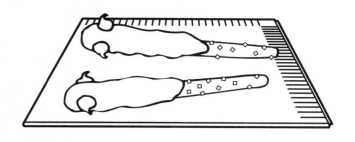

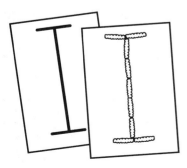

Inch by Inch

By Leo Lionni

After sharing this story of a clever inchworm, encourage youngsters to closely examine Lionni's illustrations. Point out the different textures and patterns in the art. Then provide a variety of green papers, such as wrapping paper, tissue paper, and wallpaper. Have youngsters tear strips of paper and glue them to a sheet of blue construction paper to create grassy scenes reminiscent of Lionni's style. Then have each child glue a one-inch length of pipe cleaner—an inchworm—somewhere on his picture.

Inchworm Booklet

Page by page and inch by inch, this little booklet will have your students learning about the letter *Ii*! To prepare, duplicate pages 63–66 for each child. Working with one small group at a time, have each youngster color and personalize his booklet cover and color the worms on each booklet page. Then have him cut apart the cover and pages and staple them together. Next, direct him to color and cut out the *I* pictures. Have him glue the pictures to the corresponding pages. Read the completed booklets aloud as a group.

Inchworm's Favorite Measuring Books

How Big Is a Foot? by Rolf Myller
Measuring Penny by Loreen Leedy
Twelve Snails to One Lizard: A Tale of Mischief and Measurement
  by Susan Hightower

More Inchworm and *I* Activities

- How many inches tall are your kids? Measure each child and record her height in inches on an index card. Post all the cards on a classroom wall, each one at the corresponding height.

- For each child, pencil a large letter *I* on a sheet of construction paper. Provide a large supply of green pipe cleaners cut into one-inch lengths. Encourage your students to glue the fuzzy little inchworms to the letter *I*.

I   i

inchworm

The inchworm is measuring...

Inchy Inchworm Measures

Name _____

Inchy Inchworm measures an ice skate.

1

Inchy Inchworm measures an igloo.

2

Inchy Inchworm measures an invitation.

3

Inchy Inchworm measures an icicle.

4

Inchy Inchworm measures some instruments.

5

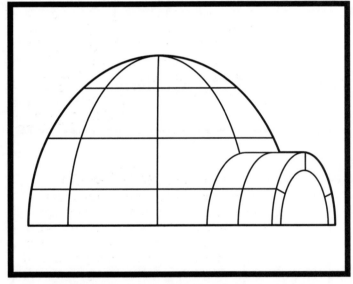

You're
Invited!

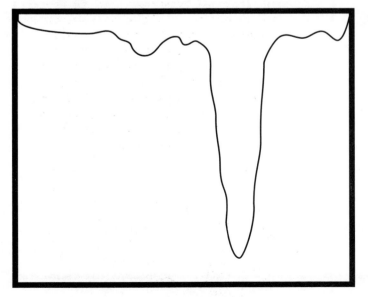

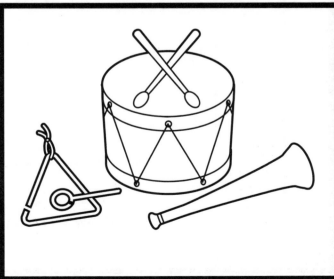

J Is for Jelly Bean

Jump right into these jazzy jelly bean activities to learn about the letter J!

Five Little Jelly Beans

Duplicate the bowl and jelly bean patterns (page 69) onto tagboard; then cut them out. Use the jelly bean pattern to trace five jelly beans, each on a different color of construction paper. Cut out the jelly beans and laminate all the pattern pieces. Cut a slit along the dotted line of the bowl. Then prepare each piece for flannelboard or magnetboard use. Use the pieces as you read the rhyme below. Then invite students to do the same!

Five little jelly beans were jiggling in a bowl.
The first one said, "Watch me! I'm gonna roll!"
The second one said, "Oh, no! I'm rolling too!"
The third one said, "Then I'm rolling on with you!"
The fourth one said, "Please don't leave me back!"
The fifth one said, "Or I'll be someone's snack!"
So they rolled and they jiggled, and they jiggled and they rolled,
Till all that was left was the jelly bean bowl!

Jelly Beans for Sale
By Bruce McMillan

The mouthwatering jelly bean photographs in this book tempt students to learn the values of coins before you even know it! After sharing the book with your students, put it in your math center along with a bowl of "working" jelly beans and a supply of coins (see below). Also provide a bowl of "snacking" jelly beans for a job well done. Invite children to read the book and use the working jelly beans and the coins to follow along with the book. Sweet!

Coins:	Jelly beans:
25 pennies	5 orange jelly beans
3 nickels	5 pink jelly beans
2 dimes	10 white jelly beans
1 quarter	15 brown jelly beans
	20 yellow jelly beans
	20 blue jelly beans
	20 green jelly beans
	20 red jelly beans
	25 purple jelly beans

Jelly Bean Book Page

Use the *J* book page on page 70 as directed for the letter *A*. Ask each child to make up a pretend jelly bean flavor and color her jelly bean accordingly. Invite her to use other art supplies to embellish her jelly bean if desired. Then have her write or dictate about her newly created jelly bean to complete the story starter. Foster a connection between home and school by giving each jelly bean–flavor inventor a copy of the award on page 69 to take home.

Ask me about my new jelly bean flavor!

Jeweled Jelly Beans

These art projects look like jeweled jelly beans when they're displayed in your sunny classroom windows! In advance, cut out two identically sized, waxed paper jelly bean shapes for each child. Also provide a variety of colorful tissue paper scraps, water-diluted glue, scissors, and paintbrushes. Have each child cut a supply of tissue paper into small pieces. Then have him paint a section of his jelly bean with glue and press on pieces of tissue paper. Have him repeat the process until the whole jelly bean is covered. Finally, instruct him to paint another coat of glue over the whole shape. Then have him press on the remaining waxed paper jelly bean. When the glue is dry, have each child trim around his jelly bean if necessary.

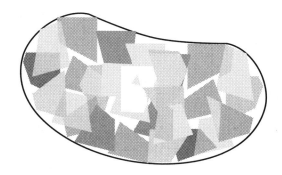

Jigsaw and Jelly Beans

These particular jelly beans encourage counting, visual discrimination, a sense of accomplishment, and fine-motor fun! In a center, set out a bowl of jelly beans and a jigsaw puzzle. Encourage students to work on the puzzle during predetermined center times. For each piece a child fits into the puzzle, have her take (and set aside) one jelly bean. When she is finished working on the puzzle for that period of time—and *before* she eats her jelly beans—have her count the jelly beans and write the total in a designated place on your chalkboard. At the end of each day, discuss the numbers on the board. Before you know it, the puzzle will be completed! What an accomplishment!

Jazzy J Cakes

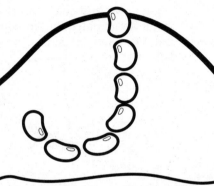

Here's just the thing to top off your study of the letter *J*—*J* cakes! In advance, bake a class supply of cupcakes. Set them out along with a container of frosting and a supply of small jelly beans. Invite each child to frost a cupcake and then use the jelly beans to make a *J* in the frosting. Just jazzy!

Another Jelly Bean Book

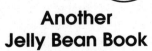

The Jelly Bean Fun Book
by Karen Capucilli

My Jelly Bean Journal

Jumping jelly beans! Look at all these *J* words! For each child, duplicate page 71 on construction paper and pages 72–73 on regular copy paper. Have each child color the bowl of jelly beans and then cut around the bold outline. Next, have him color and cut apart the *J* booklet pages. Then instruct each child to sequence the booklet pages and staple them onto the jelly bean bowl where indicated. Encourage children to read their jelly bean journals aloud together.

Savor the Flavor

Thinking caps and each child's sense of taste and sight are required for this small-group activity. Purchase a brand of jelly beans that indicates which flavor corresponds to each color (such as Jelly Belly®). Give each child in a small group the same color jelly bean, and invite everyone to look at her jelly bean and taste it. Then ask each child to guess the flavor of the jelly bean. Continue the activity, using less common flavors as you go. What fun!

More J and Jelly Bean Activities

- Fill a small jar with jelly beans and place it in your math center. Have each child guess how many jelly beans are in the jar and then write his guess on a chart. During a group time, count the jelly beans together. Any surprises? Give one clean jelly bean to each child who participated.

- Use jelly beans for color-sorting activities and as math manipulatives.

Use the bowl and the jelly bean with "Five Little Jelly Beans" on page 67.
Use the award with "Jelly Bean Book Page" on page 67.

bowl

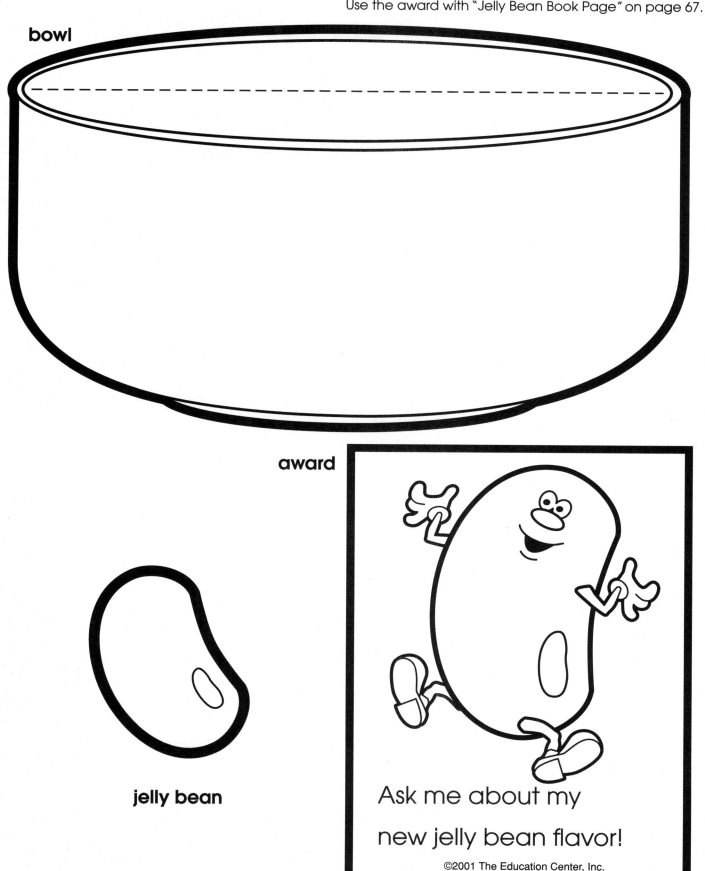

award

jelly bean

Ask me about my

new jelly bean flavor!

©2001 The Education Center, Inc.

J j

jelly bean

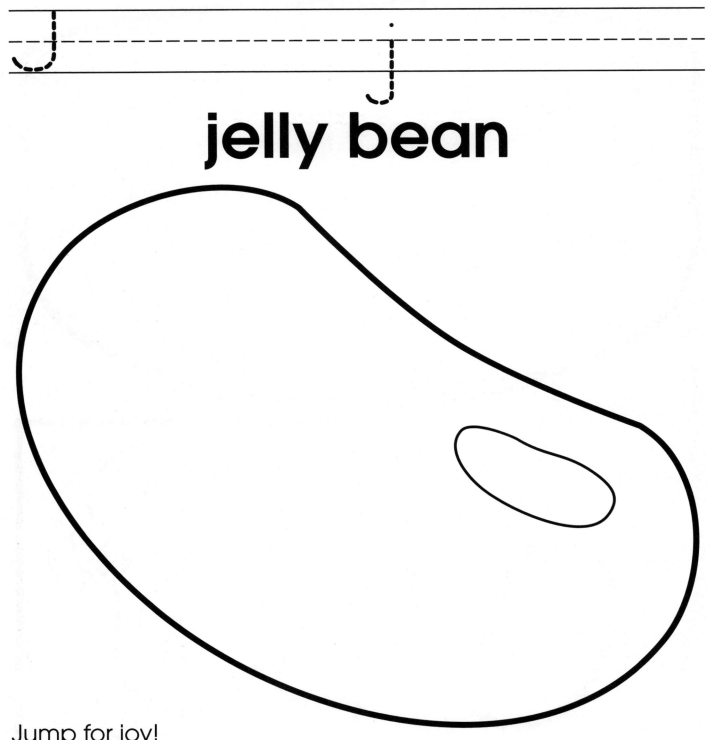

Jump for joy!

I created a new jelly bean.

It is…

Staple booklet pages here.

Booklet Cover and Pages

Use with "My Jelly Bean Journal" on page 68.

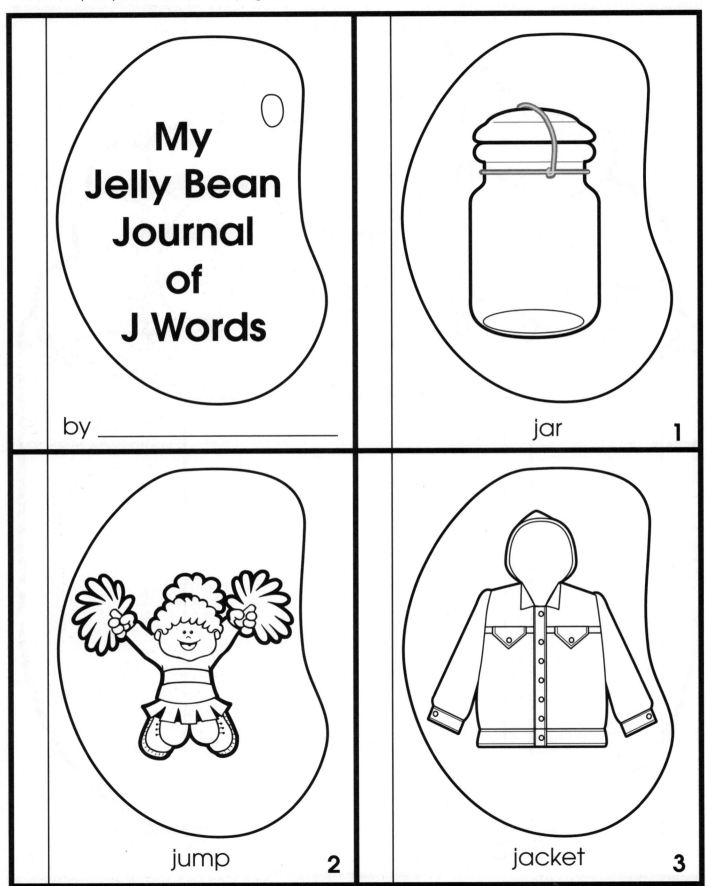

My
Jelly Bean
Journal
of
J Words

by _____

jar   1

jump   2

jacket   3

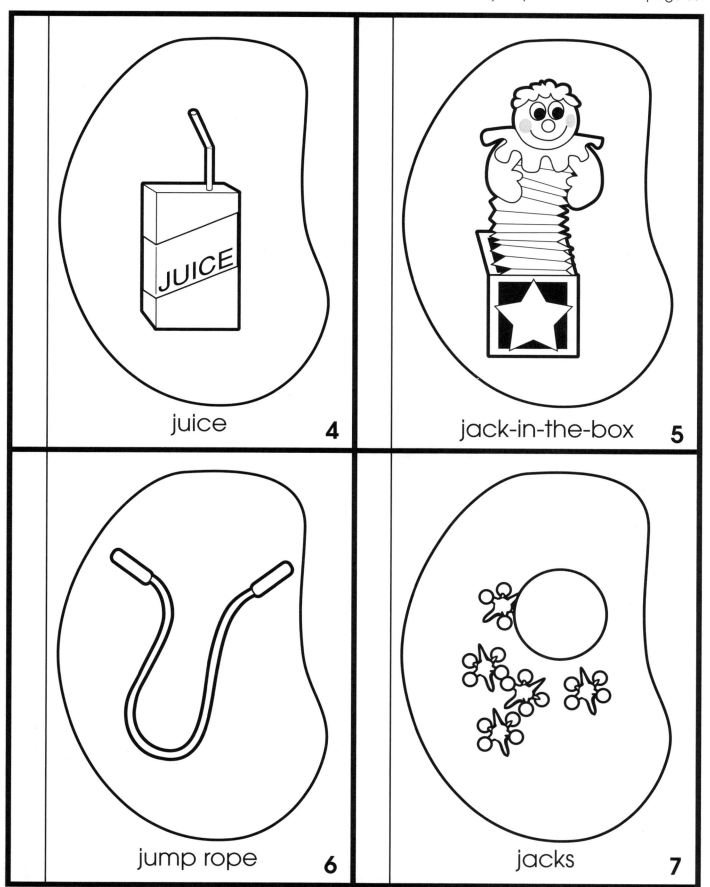

juice **4**

jack-in-the-box **5**

jump rope **6**

jacks **7**

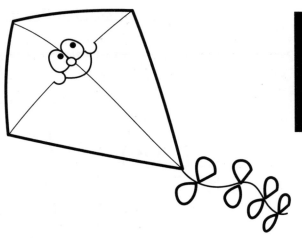

K Is for Kite

Fly up high to learn about the letter K!

If I Were a Kite

Encourage your students to make up motions to accompany the following rhyme.

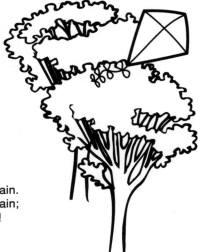

If I Were a Kite

If I were a kite,
I would fly so high.
I would fly so high
That I'd touch the sky!

If I were a kite,
I would fly over a tree.
I would fly over a tree;
Then I'd fly out to the sea!

If I were a kite,
I would zigzag through the rain.
I would zigzag through the rain;
Then I'd hide under a plane!

If I were a kite,
I would fly down to the ground.
I would fly down to the ground;
Then I wouldn't make a sound!

A Kite Bite

Have a little bite…of a kite! To make a kite snack, cut a kite shape from an unrolled fruit-roll snack. Make a small slit in the top and bottom of the kite; then slide a small straw through the slits. Fill a clear plastic cup with prepared blue gelatin. Top the gelatin with whipped topping clouds; then insert the straw through the clouds and gelatin. A nice windy-day snack!

Kite Book Page

Use the *K* book page on page 77 as directed for the letter *A*. (If desired, stir your youngsters' imaginations by sharing *One Seal* by John Stadler.) Encourage each child to think of a faraway place to which his kite might fly. Then have the child write or dictate to complete the story starter and then illustrate his work.

"K-K-K-Kite!"

Here's a learning center idea that's designed to reinforce the *K* sound. To prepare, photocopy the kite patterns (page 76) onto tagboard. Color and cut out the pictures; then laminate each kite. Complete the kites by gluing a ribbon tail onto each one. Next, program each of five small clothespins with the letter *K*. Place the kites and the clothespins in a center along with a supply of paper and various writing utensils. To do this activity, have a child clip a clothespin onto each picture that has a name beginning with *K*. To extend this activity, invite each child to illustrate and label one of the *K* words.

Kite Tails

Literacy skills fly high with this kite activity! In advance, make a class supply of the kite pattern on page 78 and the kite tail picture strips on page 79. Invite each child to color and cut out her patterns. Have her glue the picture strips together where indicated. Then cut on the dotted lines of each child's kite. Slide the picture strip through the opening as shown. Then encourage each child to pull the strip up and down, reading the *K* words as she goes.

If it flis on a lin it is calld a Kite.

Catch the Wind! All About Kites
By Gail Gibbons

• This fact-filled book will raise curiosity! (Be sure to preview this book before sharing it with your students so you can paraphrase some of the lengthier text.) After sharing the book, ask children to tell what they learned from the book. Write their responses on chart paper. Then give each child a kite-shaped sheet of paper. Ask him to illustrate something about kites that he finds interesting. Cut out two construction paper covers and title one of them "Did You Know?" Then staple all the children's pages between the covers. During a group time, invite each child to share his page.

• In advance, reproduce the kite pictures on pages 79 and 80. Color the pictures and cut them out. Make a graph by gluing a different kite picture to the bottom of each column of an eight-column chart titled "All Kinds of Kites." Review the types of kites presented in the book. Then ask each child to choose which kite she likes the best and write her initials in that column of the chart. Which kite flies highest in your class?

Flying Fish
These special kites will look beautiful flying around your schoolyard or suspended from your classroom ceiling. For each child, fold a sheet of tissue paper in half. Cut out a fish shape from both thicknesses of tissue paper. (Or have older children cut out their own shapes.) Invite each child to use markers to decorate her fish cutouts as she likes. Then cut out a 3" x 12" strip of sturdy construction paper. Roll the strip into a cylinder and staple it together. Glue the two fish cutouts together along the outside edges, leaving the head and tail sections open. Next, glue the head to each side of the cylinder, forming a mouth opening. Cut slits in the tail to create a flowing effect. Punch a hole on opposite sides on the cylinder and tie on a loop of string. Beautiful!

Kite Literature
A Carp for Kimiko by Virginia Kroll
Lucky Song by Vera B. Williams
Moonlight Kite by Helen E. Buckley
One Seal by John Stadler

More Kite and *K* Activities

• Who wants to be the king of *K*? Everyone, of course! Cut out a large construction paper crown. Ask your students to look through magazines or old workbooks and cut out pictures that have names beginning with *K.* Then invite each child to glue her pictures on the crown. During group time, review the pictures together. We're *all* the kings of *K!*

• Promote the idea of symmetry with kites. Fold a sheet of construction paper in half lengthwise. Then cut out half a kite shape on the fold. Open the kite and drop a few sparse dollops of tempera paint on one side of the kite. Fold the kite and press on the paper to spread the paint. Open up the kite for a high-flying display of symmetry! Add a crepe paper tail and display the kites on a bulletin board with a sky and cloud background.

Kite Patterns

Use with "K-K-K-Kite!" on page 74.

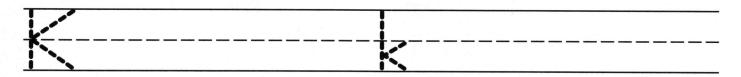

kite

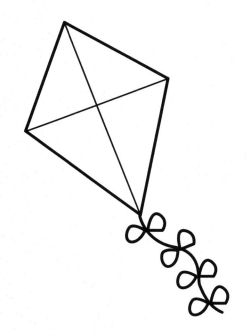

Can you see my kite?

It flew all the way to...

K
is for kite
and...

picture strips
Use with "Kite Tails" on page 74.

kite pictures
Use with *Catch the Wind! All About Kites* on page 75.

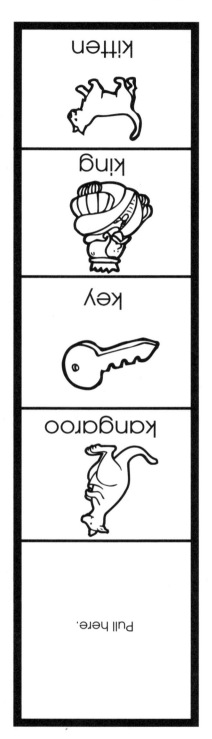

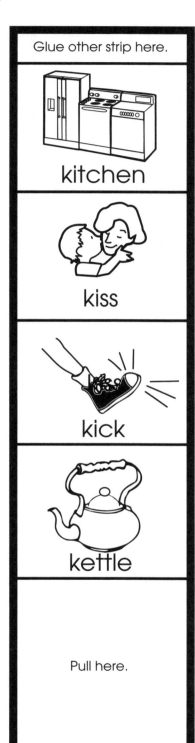

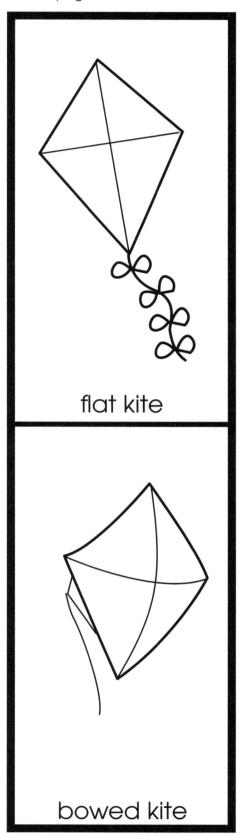

flat kite

bowed kite

Kite Pictures

Use with *Catch the Wind! All About Kites* on page 75.

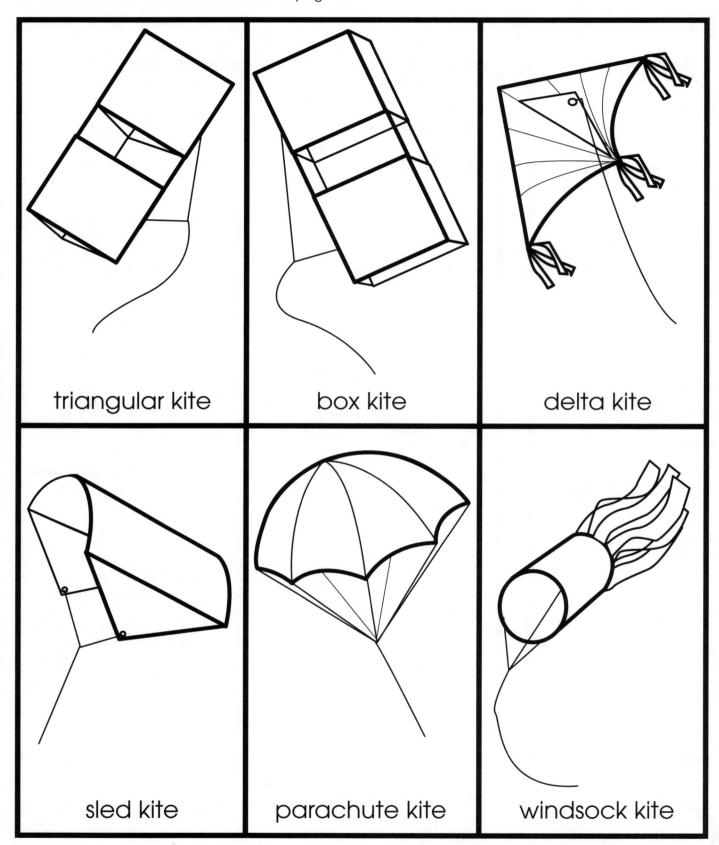

triangular kite

box kite

delta kite

sled kite

parachute kite

windsock kite

L Is for Lizard

Your little learners will love these lizard-related L activities.

I'm a Little Lizard

Use this song to reinforce colors along with the letter *L*. To begin, copy the lizard pattern (page 87) on assorted colors of construction paper. Cut out, laminate, and prepare each lizard for flannelboard use. Each time you sing the song below, display a different lizard on the board and use that color in the song.

I'm a Little Lizard
(sung to the tune of "I'm a Little Teapot")

I'm a little lizard
Long and thin.
[Green] is the color of my skin.
I like to live outside where I can run,
Eat little bugs, and rest in the sun!

* Literature Link—*A Color of His Own* by Leo Lionni

Laughing Lizard Book Page

What's making Lizard laugh? Use the *L* book page on page 83 as directed for the letter *A*. Have each child write or dictate to complete the story starter. Then have her color the lizard and illustrate what's tickling its funny bone.

Lovely Lizards

Create lots of colorful lizards with this simple art idea! To begin, enlarge the lizard pattern (page 87); then duplicate it onto white construction paper for each child. Put the lizard patterns in your art center along with glitter crayons, watercolors, and coarse sandpaper. Instruct each child to lay her lizard over a piece of sandpaper. Then have her use firm pressure to color her lizard as desired. Afterward, have her paint a watercolor wash over her lizard. When the paint is dry, ask each child to cut out her lizard. Use these lovely lizards to create a border or a bulletin board display.

Little Lizard, Little Lizard

What do you see? Turn the wheel to find out! Make a class supply of the picture and wheel patterns (pages 84–85) on white construction paper. Have each child color and cut out the patterns; then help her cut out the opening in the picture. Use a brad to attach the wheel to the picture where indicated. Then invite each child to share her project with you, turning the wheel to show each new animal as she reads.

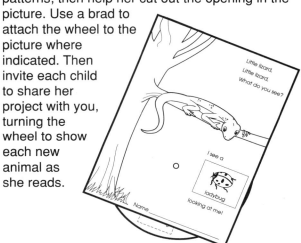

Lizard on a Log

These lazy lizards lying on logs won't last long! For each child, cut two horizontal slices from the wide end of a celery stick. Also cut a thin vertical strip about three inches long. Provide each youngster with the celery pieces, a pretzel rod, and peanut butter. To make a log, each child spreads peanut butter on his pretzel rod. Then he lays his two celery slices (lizard legs) on the peanut butter. Next, he uses the peanut butter as glue to attach the long celery strip so that it resembles a lizard's body. Lip-smacking good!

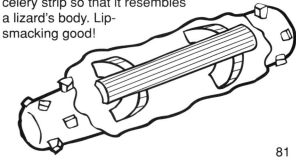

Lizard's Lollipop Booklet

Kids will love this booklet about a lucky lollipop-loving lizard. For each child, duplicate a booklet backing (page 86) and a copy of the booklet pages (pages 86–87). Also provide a lollipop and a three-inch length of pink curling ribbon. To begin, ask each child to color and cut out the backing and each booklet page. Have him tape one end of the ribbon to the lizard's mouth to resemble a tongue. Next, help him cut the slits on the backing where indicated. Then have the child slide his lollipop through the slits and secure it with tape. Finally, instruct the child to sequence and staple his pages to the backing where indicated.

Lizard Sees the World
By Susan Tews

Lizard's journey leads him to a variety of landscapes, such as a gurgling river and a rocky cliff. Invite youngsters to view the world from a lizard's perspective with this activity. Have each child fold a large sheet of white construction paper in half. Then ask her to imagine that she is a lizard and have her crawl on the ground. Invite her to illustrate the bottom half of her paper with a view from the ground. Then have her stand up tall and imagine that she is high in the sky. What does she see? Have her draw that view on the top half of her paper. Encourage each child to share her lizard-view landscapes with the class.

Lizard Literature

Amazing Lizards! by Fay Robinson
Chameleons Are Cool by Martin Jenkins
The Iguana Brothers by Tony Johnston
Lizard in the Sun by Joanne Ryder
The Mixed-Up Chameleon by Eric Carle

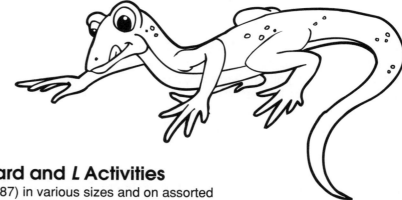

More Lizard and *L* Activities

- Copy the lizard (pattern page 87) in various sizes and on assorted construction paper colors. Cut out and laminate the patterns; then put them in a center. Invite students to sequence the lizards by size.

- Promote listening and phonemic skills with a game of Leaping Lizards! First, invite youngsters to pretend to be lizards and have them slither over to one side of the room (or behind a line if you are playing outside). To play, call out words at random. Each time you say a word beginning with the *L* sound, have each lizard leap forward. Continue play until all the lizards reach the opposite end of the room.

lizard

Look! Lizard is laughing!

He is laughing because...

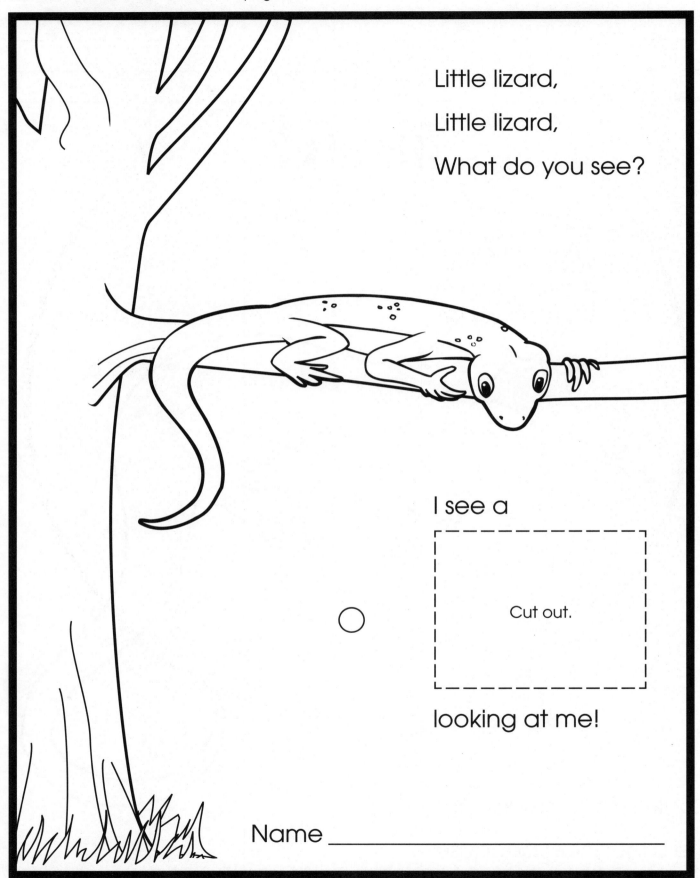

Little lizard,

Little lizard,

What do you see?

I see a

Cut out.

looking at me!

Name _____

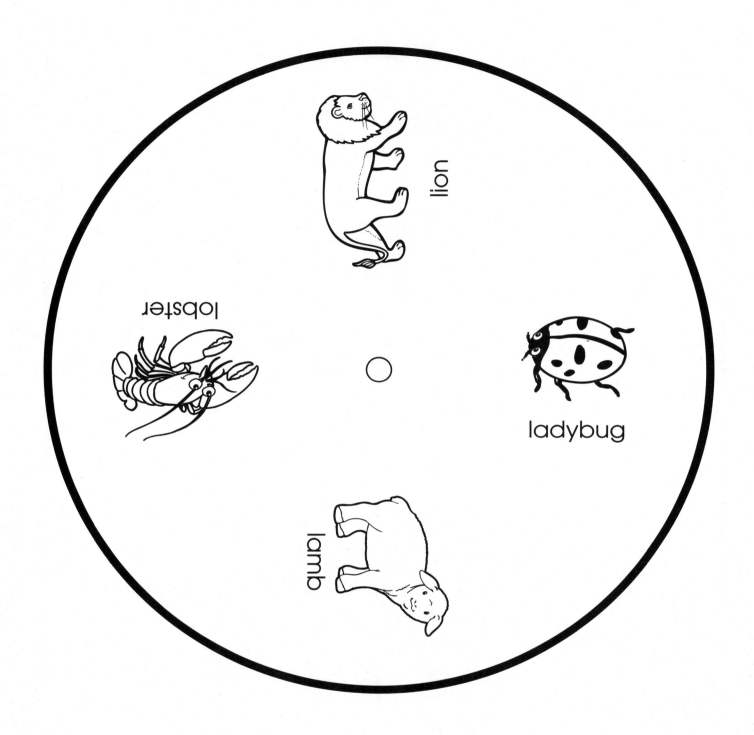

Patterns

Use with "Lizard's Lollipop Booklet" on page 82.

booklet backing

booklet pages

Lucky Lizard's Lollipops

—
—

by _____

I like a little lollipop.

1

booklet pages

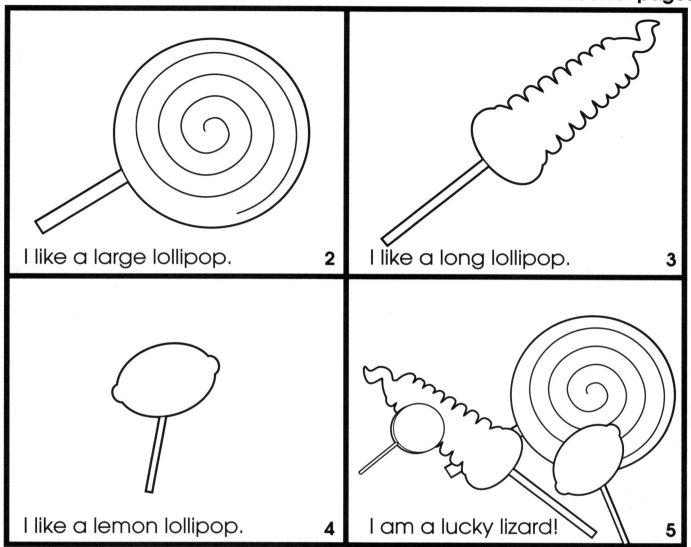

I like a large lollipop.   2

I like a long lollipop.   3

I like a lemon lollipop.   4

I am a lucky lizard!   5

lizard
Use with "I'm a Little Lizard" and "Lovely Lizards" on page 81 and
the first activity in "More Lizard and *L* Activities" on page 82.

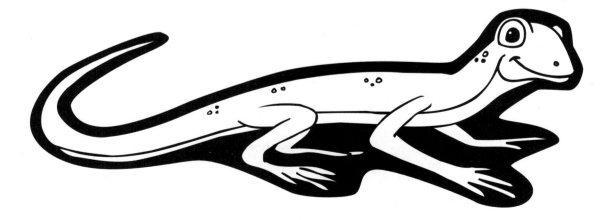

M Is for Marshmallow

Reinforce the letter M *with these mouthwatering marshmallow ideas!*

Marshmallow Book Page

Use the *M* booklet page on page 90 as directed for the letter *A*. As a class, brainstorm a list of ways to eat marshmallows. Have each child draw her favorite marshmallow treat in the space provided. Then have her write or dictate to complete the story starter.

Ways to eat
marshmallows

roasted   in s'mores
in hot cocoa   plain
in cereal   on ice cream
in peanut butter
   sandwiches

Cup o' Cocoa

Fill this cup of hot cocoa with m-m-m-marshmallows! Give each child a copy of page 91 and the top half of page 92 along with six cotton balls. Have each child glue his six cotton balls in his cup of cocoa. Then instruct each child to cut out only the marshmallows that have pictures of items  that begin with *M* on them. Have him glue each *M* picture to a cotton ball.

To make this activity into a center, enlarge and copy page 91 onto tagboard. Also copy page 92 (top and bottom halves) at its regular size onto tagboard. Color, cut out, and laminate the patterns. To do this activity, a child sorts the marshmallows and puts only those marshmallows with *M* pictures in the cup.

Marshmallow Mix

Try this easy-to-make snack that brings out the math and the marshmallow lover in each of your little chefs! In advance, make a copy of the recipe cards on page 93. Color the recipe cards; then cut them apart and mount them on a construction paper strip. Laminate the mounted recipe; then post it near your cooking area. Gather the ingredients listed below. Put each ingredient in a separate bowl and arrange the bowls for easy student access. Ready, set, cook!

Ingredients per child:
clear plastic cup
15 mini marshmallows
10 peanuts
10 raisins
10 chocolate chips

Marshmallow Masterpieces

If your students can sponge-paint, they can marshmallow-paint, too! Give each child a sheet of art paper or a large *M* cutout. Provide large and small marshmallows and several shallow trays of different colors of tempera paint. Invite each child to use the marshmallows and paint to make prints on her paper or *M* cutout. When the paint is dry, mount each project on a colorful sheet of construction paper. Marvelous marshmallow masterpieces!

The Marshmallow Song
(sung to the tune of "A Bicycle Built for Two")

Marshmallow, marshmallow,
I have to tell you, it's true.
I'm half crazy over the love of you.
I love you in my hot cocoa.
I love you roasted on fire so.
But you're the best
Besides all the rest
'tween two grahams and a chocolate bar!

Marshmallow Sundae

Here's a marshmallow counting rhyme that can go just as high as you'd like! In advance, copy the sundae bowl (page 94) onto construction paper. Also copy a supply of the marshmallows (page 94) on white construction paper. Color the sundae bowl; then laminate all the pieces. Prepare each piece for magnetboard use. To begin, place the sundae bowl and one marshmallow on the board. As you repeatedly recite the rhyme together, invite a different child each time to add another marshmallow as the rhyme indicates. Go as high as you like!

Some More S'mores

After singing "The Marshmallow Song," it goes without saying that you'll just have to make this classroom version of those irresistible campfire treats! Give each child a whole graham cracker (four sections intact). Instruct him to break his cracker in half. Then have him put a section of a chocolate bar on one half and a large marshmallow on the other. Microwave both halves on high for about ten seconds. When cool enough to handle, press the marshmallow half onto the chocolate half. But be forewarned—you just might need to make "s'more"!

Marshmallow Sundae

One little marshmallow
On my sundae.
One little marshmallow
Hoping that one day,
Another little marshmallow would come
    upon the scene,
And that little marshmallow would join
    in my ice cream!

Two little marshmallows
On my sundae.
Two little marshmallows
Hoping that one day,
Another little marshmallow would come
    upon the scene,
And that little marshmallow would join
    in my ice cream!

Three little marshmallows…

Marshmallow
By Clare Turlay Newberry

Your school or local library will most likely have this classic Caldecott Honor Book telling the story of a not-too-friendly cat and a baby bunny named Marshmallow. After sharing the book, ask children why they think the bunny is named Marshmallow. Then encourage your youngsters to share information about other animals that are named for their appearances or characteristics (for example, Midnight, Patches, Marmalade, Boots, Mocha, Bear, etc.).

Literature Link
Marshmallow Kisses by Linda Crotta Brennan

More Marshmallow and *M* Ideas

- Make marshmallow mosaics. Have each child cut out a marshmallow shape from white construction paper. Then instruct him to cut the marshmallow into little pieces. Encourage him to glue the little pieces in the shape of a marshmallow to a sheet of colorful construction paper.

- Just how does a marshmallow come to be a marshmallow? Ask each child to write about how she thinks a marshmallow is made. Bind all of the pages together with a cover titled "The Making of a Marshmallow." Invite each child to share her page with the class.

M ------- m

marshmallow

Mmm! My favorite way to eat marshmallows is...

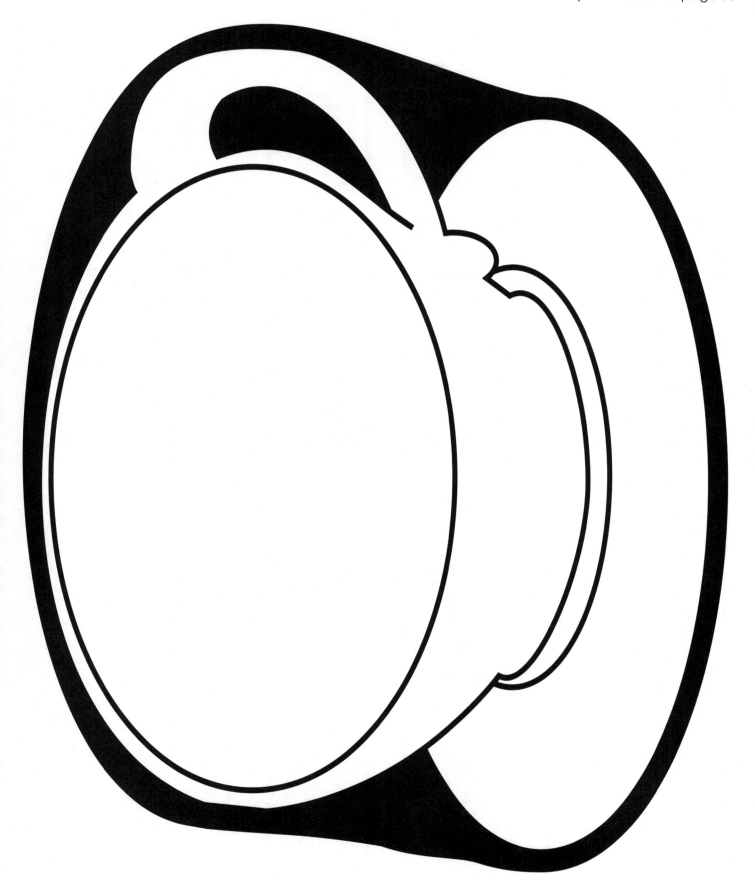

M Marshmallow Patterns
Use with "Cup o' Cocoa" on page 88.

Extra Marshmallow Patterns
Use for the center option with "Cup o' Cocoa" on page 88.

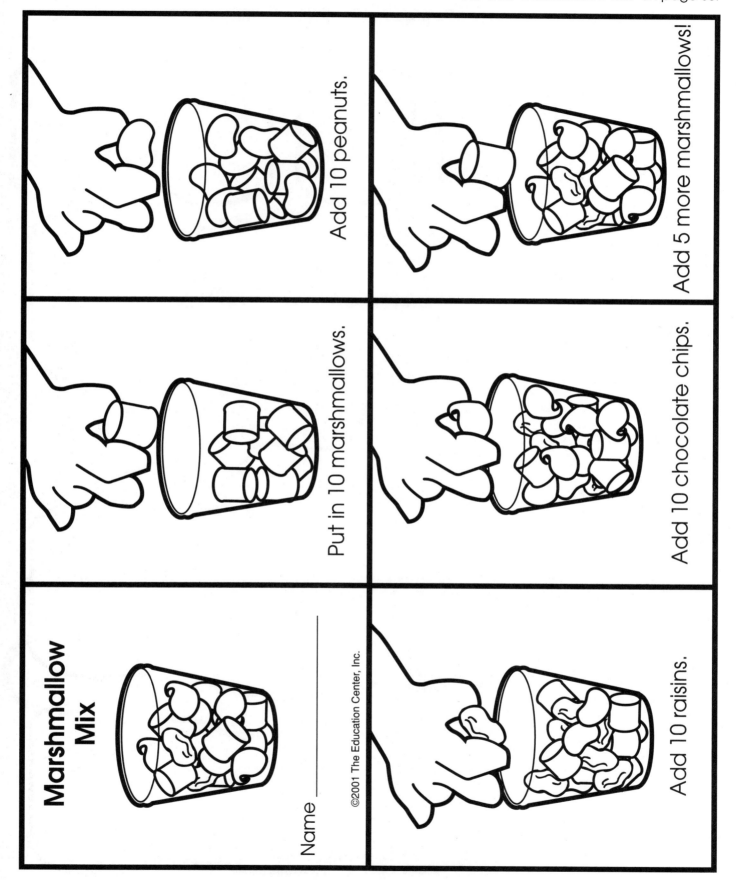

Add 10 peanuts.

Add 5 more marshmallows!

Put in 10 marshmallows.

Add 10 chocolate chips.

Marshmallow Mix

Name _____

©2001 The Education Center, Inc.

Add 10 raisins.

Patterns

Use with "Marshmallow Sundae" on page 89.

marshmallows

sundae bowl

©2001 The Education Center, Inc.

N Is for Nuts

There's "nuttin" better than these activities for teaching your little ones the letter N!

Nuts About Poetry

Teach your youngsters this poem during a group time. Then go around the circle and invite each child to name her favorite nut.

Nuts are crunchy and good to eat!
Do you like nuts for a snack or treat?
Walnuts, almonds, peanuts, too…
Which kind of nut is the nut for you?

Nutty Faces

Little ones will have a fine time creating these palatable peanut people! To make one, dip one end of a Nutter Butter® cookie into a bowl of melted white candy coating (or almond bark). Then dip the coated tip of the cookie into a bowl of crushed peanuts. Lay the dipped cookie on a piece of waxed paper. Add chocolate chip facial features. Use decorator gel to make a mouth. When the candy coating is set and your students have had a chance to show off their nutty creations, invite them to eat up!

A Snackin' Squirrel Song

Sing this song to the tune of "Five Little Ducks." Repeat the verse four times, counting down until there are "no little nuts left for his snack!" Encourage your little ones to make up motions to go along with the song.

[Five] little nuts
Grow on a tree,
Just as good as good can be.
Little squirrel comes along and…
Crack-crack-crack!
[Four] little nuts left for his snack!

Nuts Book Page

Use the *N* book page on page 97 as directed for the letter *A*. Have each child color the squirrel and draw a hiding place for the nuts. Then have him write or dictate an ending for the sentence.

The squirrel hid a big pile of nuts.
He hid them…in a tree.

A "Nut-worthy" Achievement

As your students become familiar with the letter *N*, have them participate in creating these inventive awards. For each child, duplicate the award on page 98 and the picture cards on page 99 on tan construction paper. Instruct each child to color and cut out the picture cards that show things that begin with the letter *N*. Then have her glue those pictures to the award in the spaces provided. Send the finished awards home so youngsters can show off their new knowledge to their families!

I'm nuts about the letter N! Ask me to name these pictures:

Nuts to You!
By Lois Ehlert

The mischievous squirrel in this story becomes an unwelcome visitor in the narrator's apartment. Can you guess how he gets lured back outside? After sharing the book, do the following activity to lure your youngsters to a nutty surprise *and* to help them practice following directions! To prepare, duplicate a supply of the peanut pattern on page 99. Write a clue on each peanut cutout to lead your youngsters from your classroom to various locations throughout your school—treasure-hunt-style. Provide a kid-pleasing nutty snack, such as peanut butter cookies, at the end of the trail.

Look in the cafeteria under the third window.

Books You'll Be Nuts About!

Chipmunk at Hollow Tree Lane by Victoria Sherrow
Hopper's Treetop Adventure by Marcus Pfister
Koi and the Kola Nuts by Verna Aardema
Someday a Tree by Eve Bunting

A "Wheel-y" Nutty Project

Little ones will scamper right over to make this spin-and-match project. For each child, duplicate the squirrel top sheet on page 100 and the wheels on page 101 on white construction paper. Cut out the acorn shapes on each top sheet. Next, have each child color the top sheet and cut out the two wheels. Then help her use brads to attach the wheels where indicated. Show her how to spin the wheels to match the pictures and words.

Nutty Art

Crack open some peanuts; then use the shells for a nifty letter *N* project. For each child, draw a large letter *N* on a sheet of construction paper. Then have each youngster glue peanut shell halves along the lines of his *N*.

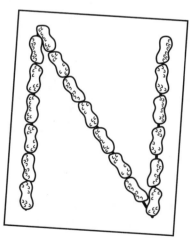

More Nuts and *N* Activities

- Encourage students to match nuts to numbers in a math center. Write the numerals 1 to 10 on separate index cards and fill a large bowl with an assortment of nuts. Have a child count out nuts to match the number on each card.

- For a fun letter *N* snack, give each child **n**ine **n**uts to **n**ibble—and serve the **n**uts on a **n**apkin.

N n

nuts

The squirrel hid a big pile of nuts.

He hid them...

Peanut Pattern
Use with *Nuts to You!* on page 96.

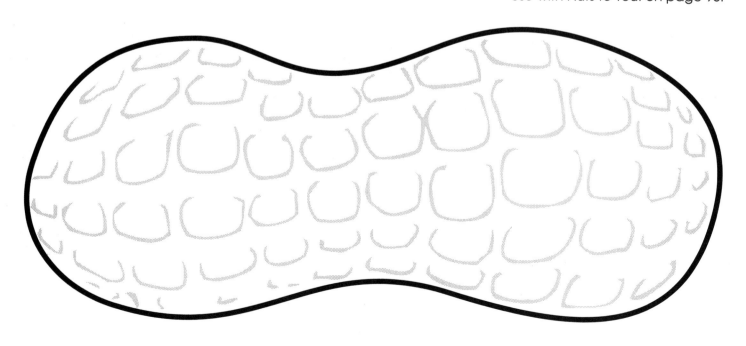

N Is for Nuts

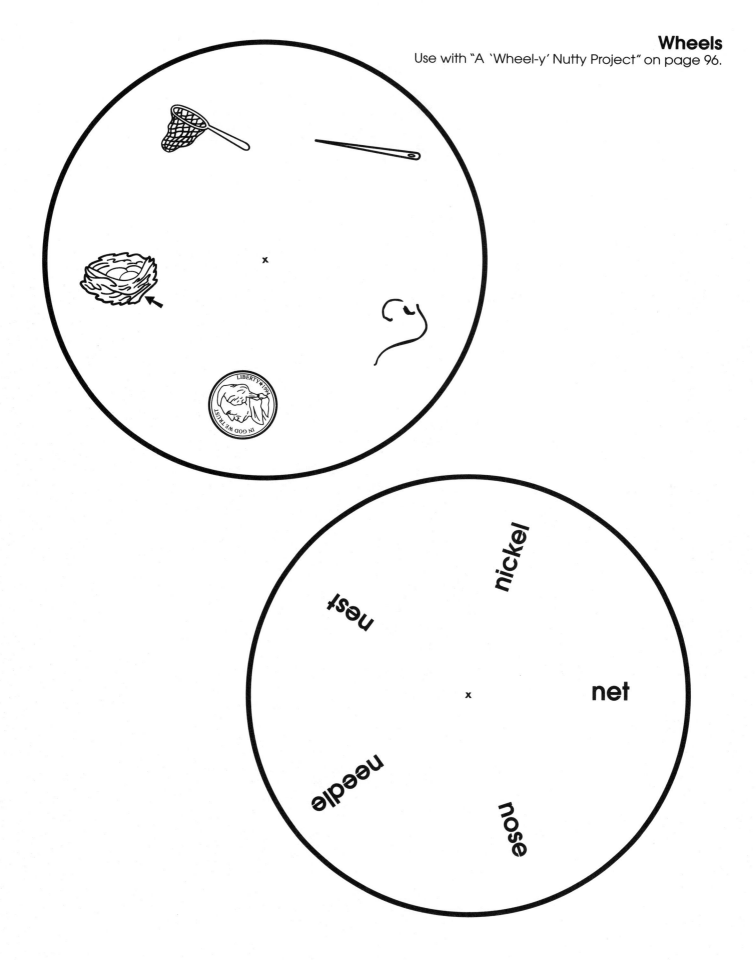

O Is for Ostrich

Get out and about with ostriches and learn about the letter O!

Odd Ostrich

Teach your class about the odd-looking ostrich with this rhyme. For additional fun, invite students to make up movements to go along with each verse.

The ostrich is an unusual bird,
So let me tell you why.
The ostrich has two little wings,
Yet he cannot fly!

His tiny head sits atop
A long and skinny neck.
He bends it to the ground, you see,
To find bugs and food to peck.

With feathers all around his body,
So big and fat and round,
He rises up on tiptoes
When he runs across the ground.

But the oddest things about the ostrich,
If I could say a little,
Are his two long, skinny legs
That bend backward in the middle!

Incredible Edible Ostriches

Invite your little ones to make these nutritious tummy fillers. To make the ostrich head and neck, each child pokes an olive onto one end of a pretzel stick. Then she pokes the neck into a peeled hard-boiled egg, the ostrich body. Next, the child pokes two half-lengths of a pretzel stick into the body to represent a sitting ostrich as shown. Then she crumbles two crackers onto a small paper plate to represent sand. Finally, the child sits her ostrich on the sand nest. Yummy!

Ostrich Book Page

Use the *O* book page on page 104 as directed for the letter *A*. This ostrich found an egg with a surprise inside! Ask each child to illustrate the surprise and then color the rest of the page. Have him write or dictate to complete the sentence.

Three-in-a-Row "Bing-*O*"

O marks the spot with this twist on the traditional bingo game. To begin, copy page 105 for each child plus one extra. Color, cut out, and laminate the extra copy of the picture cards to use as caller cards. To make the playing cards, ask each child to cut out her bingo card and picture cards. Have her color her choice of nine pictures and then glue them to her bingo card. Then invite a small group of students to play the game, using O-shaped cereal as markers. The first player to cover three pictures in a row becomes the caller for the next round of play. One, two, three in a row. "Bing-*O!*"

Ostrich's House Booklet

Open the doors in Ostrich's house to meet his oh-so-interesting animal friends! For each child, copy pages 106–108 on white construction paper. Ask each child to color his regular door pattern orange and the other doors and booklet pages as he desires. Then have him cut out all of his pages and patterns. Instruct the child to glue each door to its corresponding page (based on the booklet text). Then help him glue his pages together where indicated. When the glue is dry, have the child accordion-fold his booklet pages behind the cover. During a group time, read the booklets together; then display them standing on a flat surface.

Other Ostrich Books

Big Egg by Molly Coxe
The Lonely Lioness and the Ostrich Chicks by Verna Aardema
Ostriches (New True Books) by Emilie U. Lepthien

Zella, Zack, and Zodiac
By Bill Peet

After reading aloud this delightful tale, invite each child to create her own special ostrich. To make one, cut off the top two inches of a paper plate. Cut and decorate that smaller section to resemble an ostrich head as shown. Color the large section of the plate black to create the body. To make the neck, cut out a one-inch-wide strip from the length of a paper towel tube. Glue small pieces of cotton on the strip (neck); then glue the head to one end of it. Cut the remaining section of the tube into two ostrich legs. Color the legs; then staple the neck and legs to the body as shown. Finally, glue on white tail and wing feathers. Have each child attach her ostrich to a large paper bag so that it stands up. Then invite her to use her ostrich to retell this story or to make up her own ostrich tales. Later, have youngsters collect O-shaped items in their ostrich bags to share with the class.

More Ostrich and *O* Activities

- To create an *O* mobile, have each child color the rim of a paper plate and of several round paper doilies. Have him cut out the center of the plate and each doily. Then have him attach the doily *O*s to the paper plate *O* with tape and yarn.

- Challenge each child to use tweezers to sort the *O*s out of a supply of pasta or cereal letters. If desired, set a timer for this activity. When the timer sounds, have the child count the number of *O*s that she separated from the supply.

- Ask each child to use a circular sponge and tempera paint to print colorful circles on black paper. After the paint dries, have the child convert each circle into an *O* by filling in the center with a black marker. How many *O*s of each color does he have?

- Invite youngsters to enjoy O-shaped snacks, such as pineapple rings, olive slices, onion rings, doughnuts, or cereal *O*s.

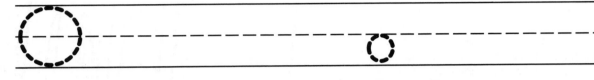

ostrich

This ostrich found a surprise inside the egg.

It was...

Three-in-a-Row Bing-O

olive	orange	ostrich	open	old
oval	otter	ox	out	over
octopus	owl	onion		

Booklet Cover and Door Patterns
Use with "Ostrich's House Booklet" on page 103.

Ostrich's House

Open the doors to meet my friends.

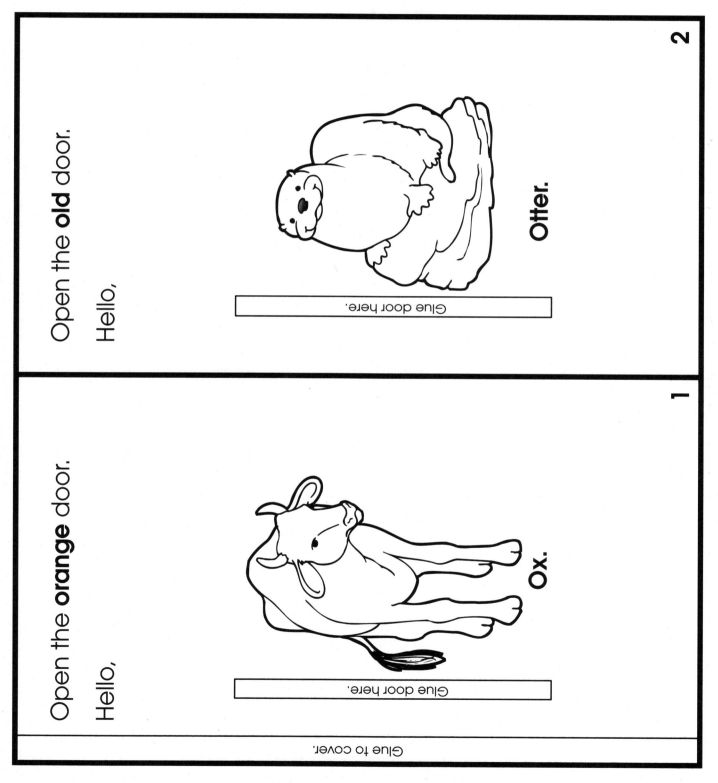

2

Open the **old** door.

Hello,

Glue door here.

Otter.

1

Open the **orange** door.

Hello,

Glue door here.

Ox.

Glue to cover.

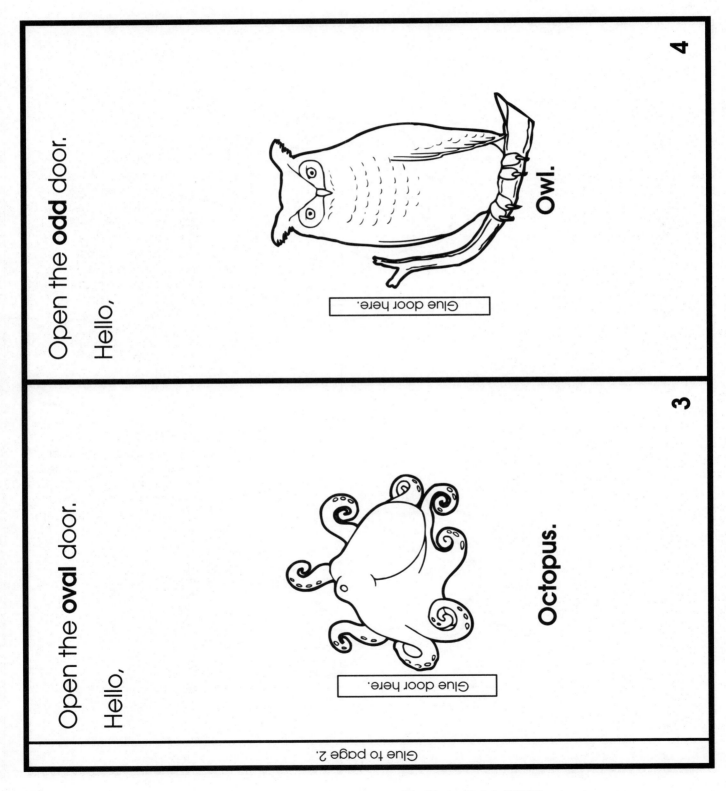

4

Open the **odd** door.

Hello,

Glue door here.

Owl.

3

Open the **oval** door.

Hello,

Glue door here.

Octopus.

Glue to page 2.

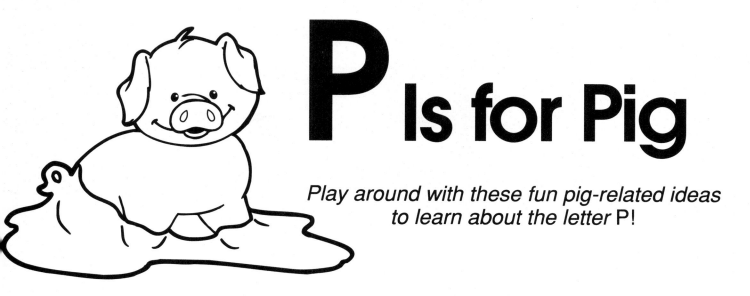

P Is for Pig

Play around with these fun pig-related ideas to learn about the letter P!

Piggy Toes

Shoes and socks can be on or off for this adapted version of an old favorite. Look for all the *P* words!

Piggy Toes
This little piggy played piano.
This little piggy painted the sky.
This little piggy played Ping-Pong®.
This little piggy baked a pie.
And *this* little piggy went pitter-patter, pitter-patter, pitter-patter…
All the way home!

* A great literature link—*The Pig in the Pond* by Martin Waddell

Pigs in a Pond

This is a very exclusive "p-p-p-pond." And why? Only pigs showing a picture beginning with the letter *P* may enter! In advance, cut out a large pond shape from blue construction paper and label it "Pigs in a Pond." Photocopy the pig pictures (pages 111–112) on construction paper. Color, cut out, and laminate each pig. Also laminate the pond. To do this activity, a child looks at each pig. If the pig has a picture beginning with the letter *P,* the child puts the pig in the pond. If not, the pig stays on the side. (If desired for self-checking, put a sticker on the back of each pig that belongs in the pond.)

Pigs on Parade

What could be better for pattern practice than *pigs!* To prepare, photocopy a large supply of the pig pictures (pages 111–112) on construction paper. (If desired, copy only the pigs with *P* pictures.) Color, cut out, and laminate each pig. Store all the pigs in a string-tie envelope. To do this activity, ask a child to arrange the pigs in a pattern parade. Then encourage him to voice the pattern: "Popcorn, popcorn, penguin" or "A, A, B."

Pig Book Page

This pig had a party to celebrate the letter *P!* Use the *P* book page on page 113 as directed for the letter *A.* As a class, brainstorm foods that begin with the letter *P.* Then have each child write or dictate to complete the story starter and then illustrate the page.

If You Give a Pig a Pancake
By Laura Numeroff

If you read this book to your children, they'll want to hear it again and again! In advance, copy the pancake pattern (page 114) 26 times on tan construction paper. After sharing the story, assign each event in the story to a different child (or small group). Have each child illustrate his assigned event on the pancake pattern and then cut out the pancake. Collect all the pictures in sequence. Then, using the illustrations one by one, invite each child to take a turn retelling part of the story.

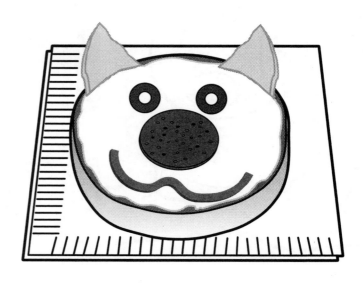

Then she will need a bath and want a toy.

More Books About Pigs

All Pigs Are Beautiful by Dick King-Smith
Five Little Piggies by David Martin
How Big Is a Pig? by Clare Beaton
The Pig in the Pond by Martin Waddell
Pigs Aplenty, Pigs Galore! by David McPhail

Pizza Pigs

These popular pizza pigs hit the spot! In advance, copy the recipe on page 115. Color and cut apart the cards; then post them in order near your cooking center. To prepare, toast an English muffin half for each child. Arrange the ingredients listed below for easy student access. Then have each child follow the step-by-step directions to make a pizza pig. Bake the pizzas at 400° until the cheese melts. Mmm—perfect!

pizza sauce
grated cheese
black olives (eyes)
pepperoni slice (nose)
strip of green pepper or carrot (mouth)
triangles cut from ham (ears)

More *P* and Pig Ideas

• For each child, draw a large *P* on a sheet of sturdy construction paper. Have each child trace the letter with a thick line of glue. Then invite each child to cover the letter with unpopped popcorn, uncooked pasta, unshelled pumpkin seeds, or a combination of all three.

• Make these see-through pouches to reinforce the letter *P.* For each day that you study the letter *P,* use a permanent marker to label a resealable plastic bag with the letter *P* and a day of the week. Tell your students that these pouches are for *P* pictures. Encourage each child to cut out or draw pictures beginning with the letter *P.* Have each child write his initials on the back of his picture and drop it into the pouch for that day. During a group time, have each child share his picture from the pouch.

Pig Pictures
Use with "Pigs in a Pond" and "Pigs on Parade" on page 109.

P   P

pig

This pig had a big party!

He served...

Pancake Pattern

Use with *If You Give a Pig a Pancake* on page 110.

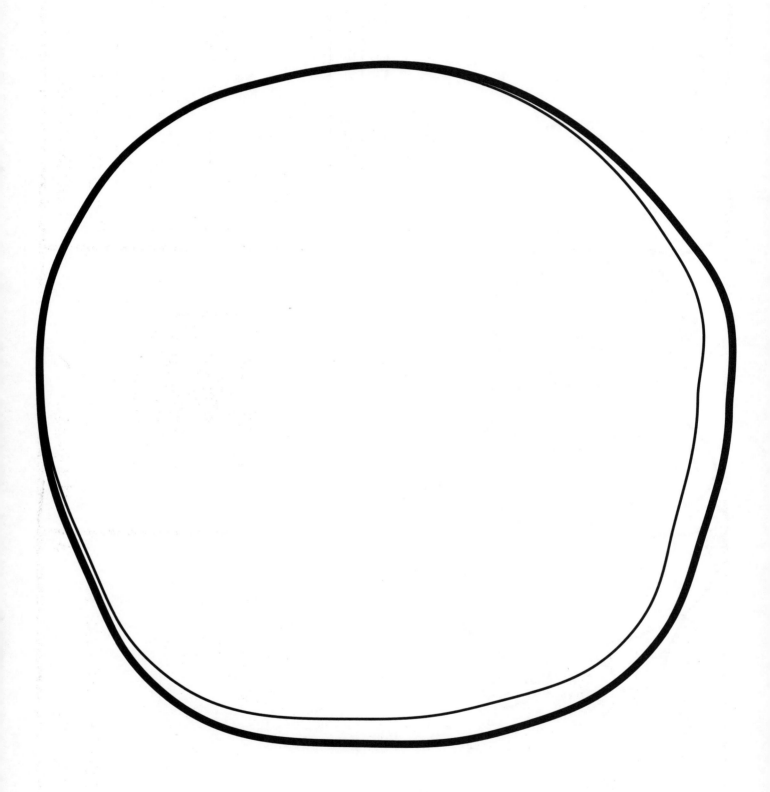

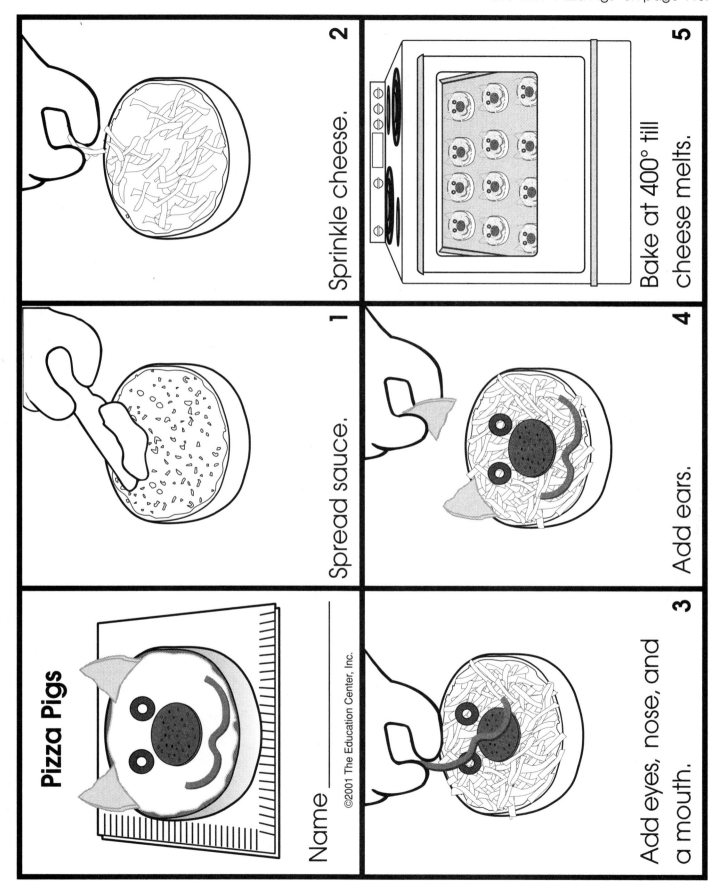

2

Sprinkle cheese.

5

Bake at 400° till cheese melts.

1

Spread sauce.

4

Add ears.

Pizza Pigs

Name _____

©2001 The Education Center, Inc.

3

Add eyes, nose, and a mouth.

Q Is for Quiet

On a quest for the best way to teach the letter Q? Let these quiet activities do it for you!

A Quiet Snack

You'll hear nary a crunch as your little ones munch this soundless snack. Before snacktime, duplicate the bag label on page 119. Invite each child to color his copy and then tape it to the front of a zippered plastic bag. Set out bowls of the ingredients listed in the recipe below, along with the proper measuring cups and spoon. Then have each child measure and mix his snack as directed on his bag label.

Quiet Mix
1/4 c. mini marshmallows
1/8 c. raisins
1 tbsp. peanut butter chips

Mix all ingredients together and chew quietly!

Sing a Quiet Song

Quietly sing this song to the tune of "Twinkle, Twinkle, Little Star."

Quiet, quiet, not a sound.
Quiet, quiet all around.
Not a whisper, not a peep;
Every noise is fast asleep.
Quiet, quiet, not a sound.
Quiet, quiet all around.

A Poem About Quiet

Teach youngsters this poem and its accompanying motions.

Quiet is the library
  (Use hands to motion opening a book.)
Or a sky of stars at night.
  (Point to sky and look upward.)
Quiet is a prowling cat
  ("Walk" hands slowly in air.)
Or a little rabbit white.
  (Put hands on head to form bunny ears.)
Quiet is a butterfly
  (Join thumbs and flutter fingers.)
Or a fish down in the deep.
  ("Swim" hand in front of body.)
Quiet is a kiss to throw
  (Throw kiss.)
Or me when I'm asleep!
  (Rest head on folded hands and close eyes.)

Paint the Q

Looking for an art project to reinforce the letter *Q?* This one qualifies! Duplicate the large letter *Q* on page 120 on white construction paper for each child. In each work area, set out a few containers of watered-down tempera paint and a large supply of Q-tips® swabs. Then play some quiet music and invite each child to work quietly as she paints her letter *Q* with Q-tips.

Quiet Book Page

Use the *Q* book page on page 118 as directed for the letter *A.* Have each child color the picture and write or dictate to complete the story starter.

The Quiet Queen's Crown

Introduce your little ones to the quiet queen and her crown of *Q* words! Duplicate the pattern of the queen on page 121 and the strip of *Q* pictures on page 119. Have each child color and cut them out. Cut along the dotted lines on each crown pattern with an X-acto® knife. Direct each child to thread the strip of pictures through the crown on her pattern. Have her pull the strip to reveal the various pictures.

Quintessential Quiet Books

A Quiet Night In by Jill Murphy
Quiet, Wyatt! by Bill Maynard
Shhhh by Kevin Henkes
Too Quiet for These Old Bones by Tres Seymour

The Very Quiet Cricket
By Eric Carle

Your students will no doubt be delighted by the chirping surprise at the end of this book. Ask them to examine the last spread of the book and to think about what the two crickets might be saying to one another. Duplicate page 122 to make a class supply. Have each youngster dictate a conversation for you to write in the speech bubbles. Have him color the page, adding a moon and stars to the sky to complete the picture.

More Quiet and Q Activities

- Have a quiet *Q* quest. Die-cut a large supply of letter *Q* cutouts and hide them all around your classroom. Invite your students to hunt for them—quietly!

- Play The Quiet Game while students are waiting in line. Ask everyone to be as quiet as possible. Tap the child you think is quietest. That child may then survey the line and tap the child she thinks is quietest. Continue as time permits.

- Designate an area of your room as the Quiet Corner. Put a cozy rug and some floor pillows there along with quiet amusements, such as puzzles, books, and playing cards.

- Make a *Q* card. Duplicate the large letter *Q* on page 120. Glue it to a small sheet of poster board. Display the *Q* card during quiet work times or hold it up briefly as a reminder when students need to be quiet.

Q q

quiet

Quentin is quiet because...

Q Picture Strip

Use with "The Quiet Queen's Crown" on page 117.

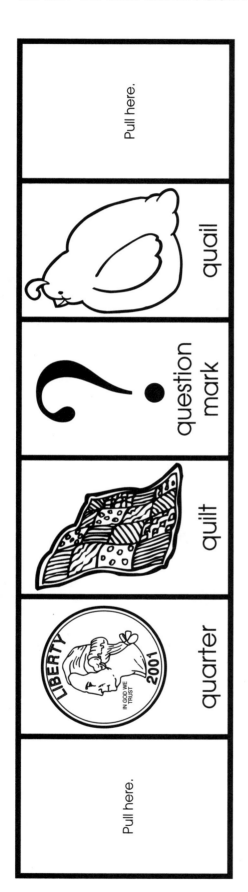

Quiet Mix

mini marshmallows

raisins

peanut butter chips

Quiet Mix

mini marshmallows

raisins

peanut butter chips

Q Pattern

Use with "Paint the *Q*" on page 116 and "More Quiet and *Q* Activities" on page 117.

A Quiet Cricket Conversation

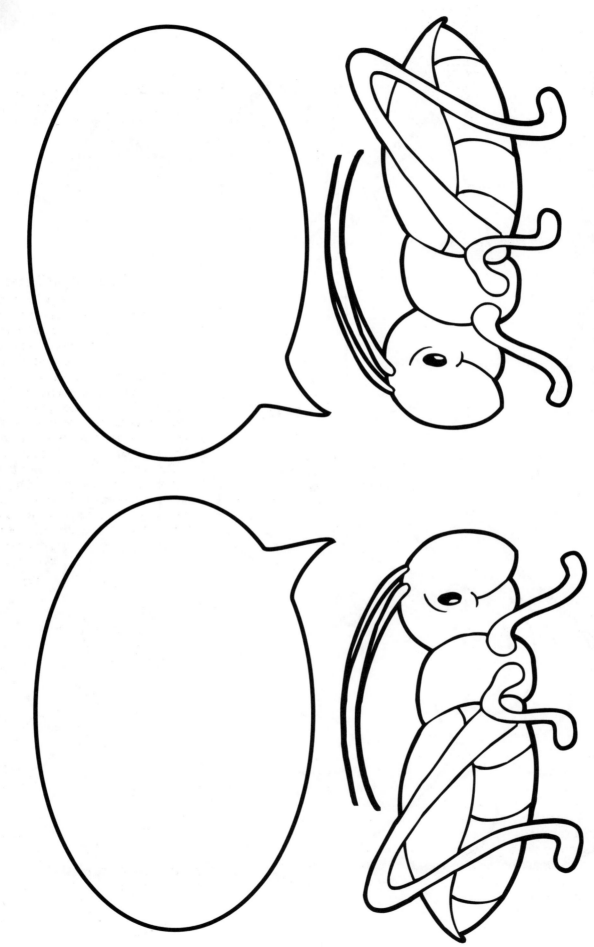

Note to the teacher: Use with *The Very Quiet Cricket* on page 117.

R Is for Rooster

Youngsters will crow with excitement over these R *ideas!*

Rooster's on the Roof

Use this rhyme to teach youngsters that farm life includes lots of activity. Each time you recite the rhyme, invite a child to pantomime a different farm activity for the class to guess.

Rooster's on the roof.
Sun's on the rise.
It's time for me
To open my eyes.

Cock-a-doodle-doo!
Oink. Baa. Moo.
Get up. Get going.
There's so much to do!

Rooster Book Page

From his roost on the rail, the rooster sees all the sights! Use the *R* book page on page 125 as directed for the letter *A*. Encourage each child to write or dictate to complete the sentence starter on the page. Then have her illustrate her writing in the space provided.

Cock-a-Doodle Stew

Invite your students to stir up some pudding stew filled with a rooster's favorite—seeds and bugs. To begin, prepare a half-cup serving of cooked instant rice for every four students. Then mix up a class quantity of instant vanilla pudding. Place the pudding on a table along with the cooled rice and containers of raisins and sunflower seeds (to represent seeds and bugs). Ask each child to spoon a serving of pudding into a bowl. Then have him stir in two spoonfuls of rice and a spoonful of raisins. Invite him to top his stew with a sprinkling of sunflower seeds. Cock-a-doodle ste-e-e-ew!

Crowing Caps

Put the crowning touch on your rooster activities with these unique caps. For each child, copy the rooster comb and wattle (page 126) on red construction paper and the beak on yellow paper. To make a cap, remove the metal strip from a disposable dust mask. Then paint the mask with brown tempera paint. When the paint dries, cut a 3-inch slit along the top as shown. Cut out the patterns; then cut the slits in the comb where indicated. Insert the comb in the slit on the mask (cap) and secure it with masking tape on the inside. Then fold the beak in half and accordion-fold the wattle. Staple the beak and wattle to the cap as shown. To complete the cap, attach two pom-pom eyes with craft glue. When the glue is dry, invite youngsters to wear their crowing caps during your *R* and rooster activities.

The Rooster's Gift
By Pam Conrad

Proud Rooster believes that he has an extraordinary gift—the ability to make the sun rise! After reading the story, ask youngsters to share their ideas about Rooster's gift. Then invite each child to make this special henhouse. To make one, color the henhouse and wheel patterns (pages 128–129), making sure to color the rooster red. Cut out the patterns and the opening in the henhouse. Use a paper fastener to attach the wheel to the henhouse where indicated. To use, each child turns his wheel so that a day of the week shows through the opening; then he reads the text and names the word on the rising sun. Each child will soon discover that his rooster does have a gift—a new *R* word to crow about each day!

Rooster Books to Crow About

Cock-a-Doodle Doo! by Janet Stevens and
   Susan Stevens Crummel
Cock-a-Doodle-Moo! by Bernard Most
How the Rooster Got His Crown by Amy Lowry
   Poole
Rooster's Off to See the World by Eric Carle

Rooster Roadster Story Cone

Reinforce lots of *R* words as youngsters travel round with the rooster roadster. For each child, copy the spinner pattern (page 127) onto tagboard and the car and picture patterns onto white construction paper. To make a cone, each child colors a paper plate green. Then instruct her to make a cut in the plate from one edge to the center. Help her form a cone by overlapping and taping a three-inch section of the rim together. Next, ask the child to color and cut out the car, the pictures, and the spinner. Have her glue each picture along the bottom edge of her cone. Then have her fold her spinner and glue her car where indicated. Finally, help the child punch a hole in the spinner and then attach it to her cone with a paper fastener as shown. To use, the child "drives" her roadster around the story cone, reading the text as she passes each picture. Hey, Rooster's really reading!

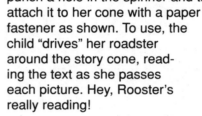

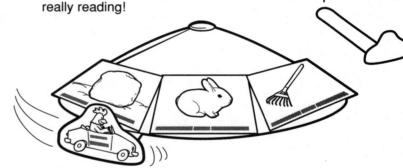

More Rooster and *R* Activities

- Have each child color and cut out the rooster, hen, and door patterns on a copy of page 126. Then have her glue them onto a letter-size envelope to create a henhouse. Ask her to draw or glue pictures of *R* words on several notecards and then insert them in her henhouse. During a group time, invite each child to share her words with the class.

- Invite youngsters to play Rooster Sees… To play, a child is assigned the role of rooster. The rooster decides on an object that is visible to his classmates and then says, "Rooster sees [color of object]." The child who correctly guesses the item becomes the next rooster.

- Pass a rock around your circle of students while playing a musical selection. After a short period, stop the music. Ask the child holding the rock to name a word beginning with *R*.

124

R - - - - - - - - - - - - - - - r - - - - - - - - - - - - - - - -

rooster

The rooster roosts on the fence. He sees...

Rooster Patterns
Use with "Crowing Caps" on page 123.

comb

wattle

beak

Patterns
Use with the first activity in "More Rooster and *R* Activities" on page 124.

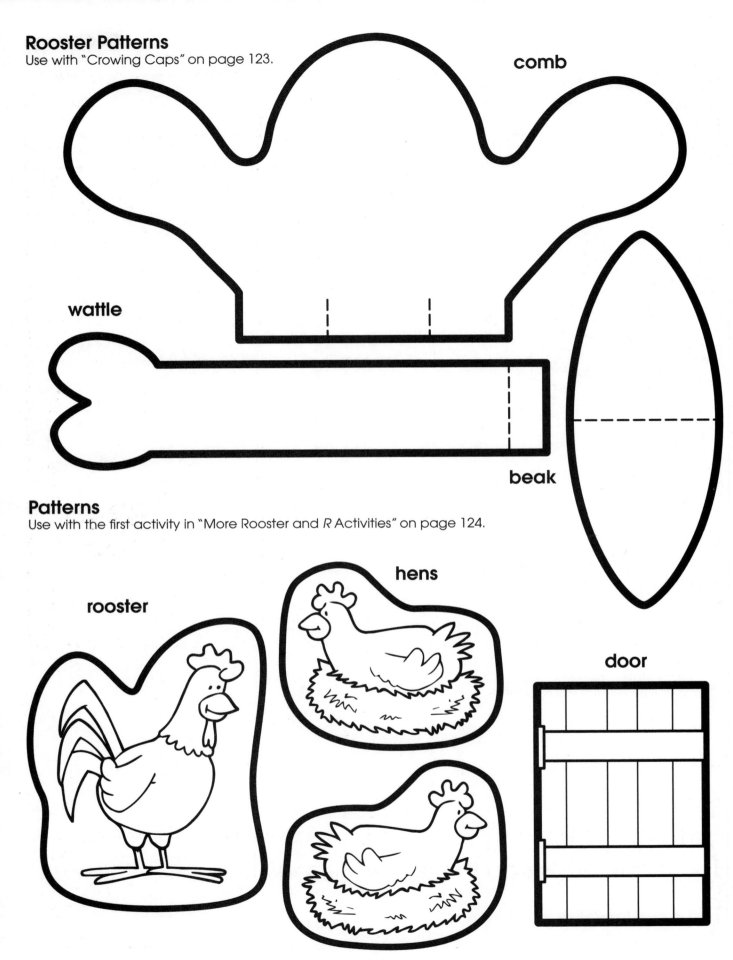

rooster

hens

door

©2001 The Education Center, Inc. • *Letter of the Week—Book 2* • TEC603

pictures

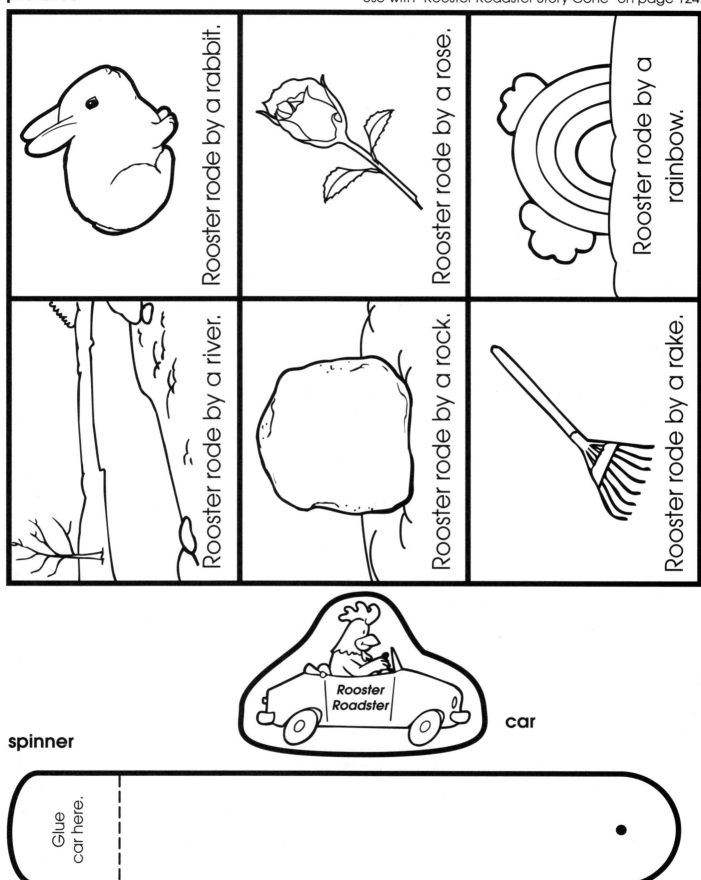

Rooster rode by a rabbit.

Rooster rode by a rose.

Rooster rode by a rainbow.

Rooster rode by a river.

Rooster rode by a rock.

Rooster rode by a rake.

Rooster Roadster

car

spinner

Glue car here.

Henhouse Pattern

Use with *The Rooster's Gift* on page 124.

Today is [   ]

What does the red rooster say?

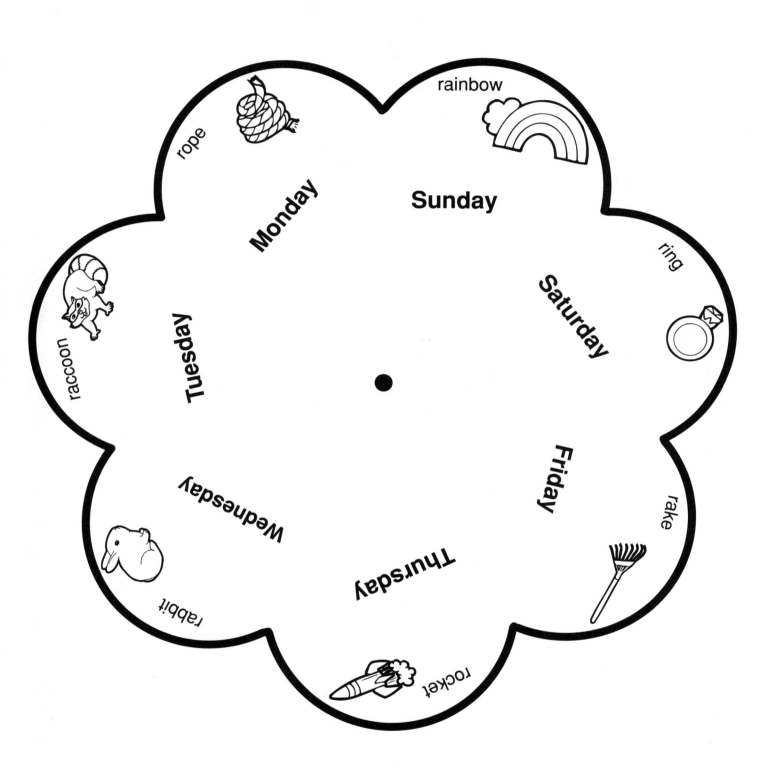

S Is for Socks

*Slip into these comfy sock activities
that reinforce the letter S!*

A Pair of Socks
By Stuart J. Murphy

A lost sock's search for its match tumbles patterning and matching skills together with a universally appealing story. To prepare, copy the sock patterns (pages 132–133) twice onto colored construction paper. Color and laminate the patterns before cutting them apart. If you don't have a dog or puppy puppet in your classroom, make a simple one by following the directions in "Sock Puppets." After sharing the story, seat your children in a circle. Spread out one set of the sock patterns. Have the puppy hold one of the socks (from the remaining set) in his mouth. Then invite your children to recite "Hello, Pup!" with you. Between the first and second stanzas, choose a child to find the matching sock to give to Pup. Then have Pup drop the pair into a basket. Repeat, letting the children take turns with Pup, until all the socks are in the basket.

Hello, Pup!

Hello, Pup!
How do you do?
We have a sock that
  belongs to you!

Here you go, Pup!
A match made for toes.
Now into the basket the
  matching pair goes.

Sock Center

For this activity, use the sock patterns made in the activity for *A Pair of Socks*. Store them in a decorated string-tie envelope. Place the envelope, a basket, and the book in a center. To do this activity, a child takes all the socks out of the envelope. As she matches each sock pair, she puts them in the basket. To add a fine-motor component, have the child clip each pair together using a mini clothespin.

Sock Puppets

Silly or serious, these sock puppets invite creative letter *S* fun! In advance, ask each child to bring a clean sock to school. Demonstrate how to slide a small paper cup into the toe of a sock; then have each child do the same. Next, demonstrate how each child can make the appearance of a mouth in his puppet by putting his fingers in the paper cup and his thumb in the heel section of the sock. Then invite children to decorate their puppets with wiggle eyes, puff paints, and other assorted craft supplies that you have on hand.

My Super Sock Book

Each of these super sock books turns out to be one of a kind! To prepare, copy the booklet pages (pages 134–135) onto construction paper for each child. Read the text together; then invite each child to illustrate her pages. Afterward, have each child cut apart her pages and sequence them. Then help each child staple the pages together. Read the books together while sitting in a circle so children can see one another's illustrations.

Sock Book Page

Use the *S* book page on page 136 as directed for the letter *A*. Talk about all the different kinds of socks. Encourage each child to illustrate his own special pair of socks—real or imaginary. (See the ideas below for some art ideas.) Then have each child write or dictate to complete the story starter.

- Place a piece of rough sandpaper or corrugated cardboard under the page; then color over it.

- Color the socks; then decorate them by gluing on buttons, sequins, or fabric scraps.

- Use rubber stamps and colorful stamp pads.

- Color the socks and then paint a thin layer of water-diluted glue over them. Sprinkle glitter over the glue. When the glue is dry, shake off the excess glitter.

Socks for Snack

Edible socks? Well, just this one time! In advance, cut out a sock shape from a large soft tortilla for each child. (You can use scissors or a cookie cutter.) Provide easy access to plastic knives, spreadable cream cheese, thinly cut vegetables, cold cuts, and cheese. Give each child a tortilla sock shape and a paper plate. Have him spread cream cheese on his sock and then use the other ingredients to decorate the rest of it as desired. You can even roll up these socks before eating them if you'd like!

S-S-S-Socks!

Fill this sock with the sound of *S!* Cut out a large sock from tagboard. Invite each child to draw or cut out pictures of things that begin with *S*. Children might also like to search their junk drawers or no-longer-used toy collections at home for small objects. During a group time, invite each child to glue his pictures or objects to the cutout. Keep on going until the sock is filled!

More Sock Selections

Caps, Hats, Socks, and Mittens by Louise Borden
Fox in Socks by Dr. Seuss
Socks by Janie Spaht Gill
Whose Socks Are Those? by Jez Alborough

Sock Patterns
Use with *A Pair of Socks* and "Sock Center" on page 130.

©2001 The Education Center, Inc. • *Letter of the Week—Book 2* • TEC603

My
Super
Sock
Book

by _____

©2001 The Education Center, Inc.

1

This sock has one color.

2

This sock has two colors.

3

This sock has three colors.

Use with "My Super Sock Book" on page 131.

4 This sock has stripes.	5 This sock has polka dots.
6 This sock has a pattern.	7 This is my favorite sock.

S _ _ _ _ _ _ _ _ _ _ s _ _ _ _ _

socks

Socks! Socks! So many kinds of socks!

My socks are…

T Is for Tiger

Teaching T with tigers will have your students roaring for more!

Tiger Song
(sung to the tune of "Bingo")

Deep in the jungle lives a cat,
And Tiger is his name-o.
T-I-G-E-R, T-I-G-E-R, T-I-G-E-R,
And Tiger is his name-o.

As you sing the song in the same manner as "Bingo," have children growl instead of clap as a substitute for each of the letters.

Terrific Tiger Tails

Grab the tiger by the tail with this terrific tiger treat. Insert a craft stick into a banana half. Spread softened, orange-tinted cream cheese over the banana. Then wrap a long string of black licorice around the banana to create stripes. A snack to satisfy the greatest of growling tummies!

Torn-Paper Tigers

Your little ones will pounce on this art activity! For each child, provide a nine-inch paper plate, two large wiggle eyes, six white pipe cleaner pieces, scraps of black and pink construction paper, glue, and access to orange fingerpaint. To make a tiger, fingerpaint the paper plate orange. When the paint is dry, make thick stripes across the plate with glue. Cover the glue with small, torn pieces of black construction paper. Tear two large ear shapes from black construction paper and glue them onto the rim of the plate. Then tear a nose from pink construction paper and glue it onto the center of the plate. To complete the tiger, glue on the wiggle eyes and pipe cleaner whiskers.

The Tiger Tango

Have your students form a circle and then move and groove to the following verses adapted from the traditional tune of "The Hokey-Pokey."

You put your right paw in.
You take your right paw out.
You put your right paw in;
Then you shake it all about.
You do the Tiger Tango,
And you turn yourself around.
That's what it's all about!

Additional verses:
You put your left paw in…
You put your sharp teeth in…
You put your long tail in…
You put your striped self in…

Tiger Book Page

Use the *T* book page on page 139 as directed for the letter *A*. Encourage each child to think of a name that begins with *T* for his tiger. Help him write that name in the blank. Then have the child write or dictate to complete the story starter and then illustrate his work.

Tiger Foldout Book

This tiger book will suit your youngsters to a T! To prepare, duplicate pages 140 and 141 on white construction paper for each child. Have each child color the tiger front and back pieces and cut them out. Then have him cut out the two book page strips along the bold outlines. Show the child how to glue the tiger covers and the booklet pages together. Next, have him color the *T* picture cards, cut them out, and glue them to the corresponding pages of the book. Fold the book accordion-style, so that the tiger pieces meet. "*T*-riffic"!

Who Is the Beast?
By Keith Baker

Your young readers will meet a tiger—piece by piece—in this lushly illustrated book. Follow up by having your students put together tiger puzzles—piece by piece. For each child, duplicate the tiger puzzle on page 142 on white construction paper. Encourage each student to color her tiger. Then have her cut apart the pieces of the puzzle on the bold lines. Have her label the back of each puzzle piece with her initials to prevent any mix-ups. Provide each child with a zippered plastic bag for storing her puzzle pieces. Then invite her to assemble the puzzle.

Terrific Tiger Tales

Horace by Holly Keller
I Don't Want to Go to Bed! by Julie Sykes
My G-r-r-r-eat Uncle Tiger by James Riordan
Tickling Tigers by Anna Currey

More Tiger and *T* Activities

- Duplicate the tiger-striped letter *T* on page 143 for each child. Encourage her to color her *T* orange with black stripes.

- In your writing center, invite children to compose some tiger tales! Provide inspiration by displaying pictures of tigers and labeling sentence strips with words your students might want to write, such as *tiger, stripes, roar,* and *jungle.*

- Have your little ones pretend to be tigers on the prowl. What are they hunting for? Letter *T*s, of course! Die-cut a supply of *T*s and hide them around your classroom. Then set your wild tigers loose to hunt for them. Encourage each tiger to roar when he makes a catch!

- Set out the materials for making tiny tigers at your art center. Provide white paper, an orange ink pad, and some fine-tipped black markers. Have each little artist make orange fingerprints on the paper; then have her use a black marker to add facial features, ears, and stripes to transform her fingerprints into tiny tigers!

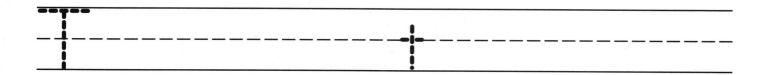

tiger

This tiger's name is _____.

He wears a T-shirt when...

Patterns
Use with "Tiger Foldout Book" on page 138.

picture cards

tiger front and back pieces

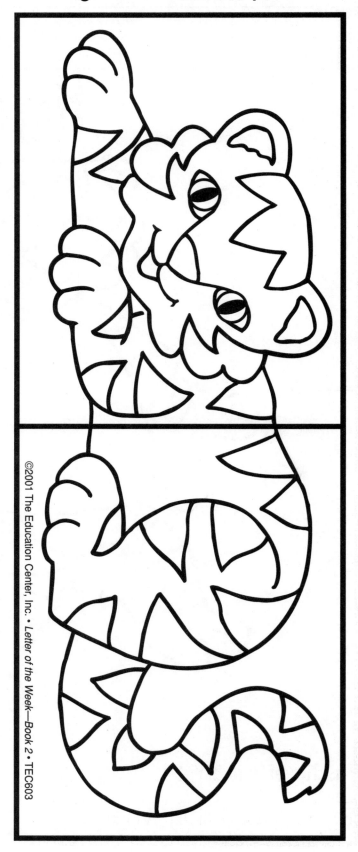

©2001 The Education Center, Inc. • Letter of the Week—Book 2 • TEC603

Glue to the back of the tiger.

turtle

tire

Glue to the other strip.

tent

table

Glue to the front of the tiger.

Tiger Puzzle
Use with *Who Is the Beast?* on page 138.

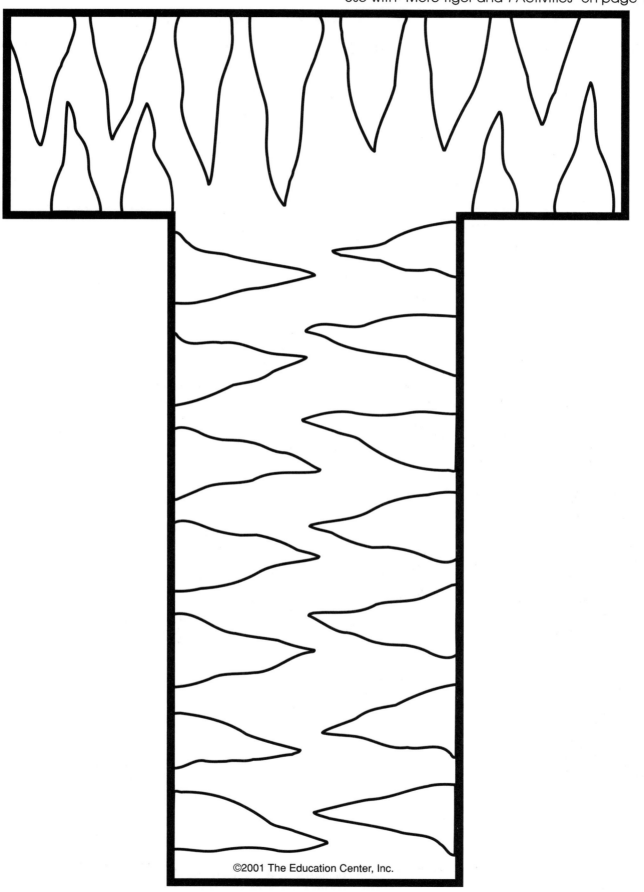

©2001 The Education Center, Inc.

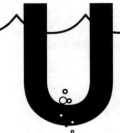

U Is for Underwater

Dive into these ideas for teaching the letter U!

Sea Sipper

The secret to this simple snack is the presentation! Give each child a clear plastic tumbler and some fish and shell stickers. Have each child attach the stickers to the outside of her cup. Then pour blue Kool-Aid® into each cup. Invite your little ones to drink in the resulting underwater scene—first with their eyes, then with their mouths! (Best when served with fish-shaped crackers.)

An Underwater Tune

Sing this song to the tune of "For He's a Jolly Good Fellow." Each time you repeat it, invite a student to name a different sea creature to substitute for the underlined word.

Let's dive underwater!
Let's dive underwater!
Let's dive underwater!
Maybe we'll see [a shark].

Maybe we'll see [a shark].
Maybe we'll see [a shark].
Let's dive underwater!
Maybe we'll see [a shark].

Underwater Book Page

Use the *U* book page on page 146 as directed for the letter *A*. Encourage each child to color the swimmer to resemble himself. Then have him write or dictate to complete the story starter and draw something he might see underwater.

Underwater Poetry

Teach your little underwater explorers this poem and its accompanying motions.

Let's go underwater!	*Hold nose and wriggle down to floor.*
Come swim with me!	*Make swimming motions.*
What kind of creatures	*Gesture "what?"*
Will we see?	*Shade eyes with hand.*
A little fish? A shark?	*Use thumb and forefinger to indicate "small."*
	Make biting motion with hand.
Maybe a whale!	*Put arms out to sides to indicate "big."*
Watch out, now,	*Rest right elbow on left hand;*
For that great big tail!	*sway right forearm back and forth.*
Look! There's a turtle!	*Point to left.*
Look! There's a skate!	*Point to right.*
I see an octopus	*Shade eyes with hand.*
With his arms—all eight!	*Hook thumbs together; wiggle eight fingers.*
We're underwater,	*Hold nose and wriggle down to floor.*
Swimming in the sea.	*Make swimming motions.*
Won't you come along	*Gesture "come on!"*
And swim with me?	*Make swimming motions.*

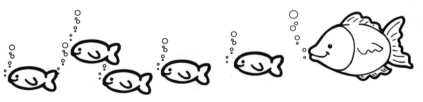

Are *U*s Under There?

Send your underwater explorers on a hunt for *U* words. To prepare, tint the water in your water table blue. Duplicate the pictures on page 147. Cut apart all the pictures and then laminate them, along with a large cutout of the letter *U*. Attach a paper clip to each picture (for weight); then sink all the pictures in your water table. Place the *U* cutout on a table near your water table. To use this center, a child pulls a picture from the water. He determines whether the word begins with the letter *U*. If it does, he places it on the *U* cutout. If not, he tosses it back underwater. If desired, draw five equally spaced dots on the *U* cutout. Have the child place each picture on a different dot so he'll know when he has found all the *U* pictures. As a variation, make two sets of *U* pictures and challenge youngsters to find matching pairs before stacking them on the *U* cutout.

Underwater Booklet

Invite each of your students to create a booklet about the underwater world. Duplicate the booklet cover and pages on pages 147–149 on blue construction paper. Have each child cut out her booklet cover and pages. Ask her to write her name on the cover and decorate it with drawings or fish-related stickers. Read through the text on each page together; then ask each child to illustrate her pages. When all the pages are complete, instruct each child to lay her pages in order in a line to the right of the cover. Help each child use clear tape to join the pages together, front and back. Then have her accordion-fold her booklet with the cover on top.

Sea Shapes

By Suse MacDonald

Simple shapes are transformed into a variety of ocean dwellers in this cleverly illustrated book. Encourage your little artists to make some shape transformations of their own with this art idea. Duplicate a supply of the shapes on page 150 on a variety of colorful construction paper. Have each child choose a shape to cut out and glue onto a sheet of construction paper. Then have him draw around it to create an underwater scene.

Come "Sea" These Underwater Books

Look Who Lives in the Ocean by Alan Baker
My Home Is the Sea: Who Am I? by Valérie Tracqui
My Visit to the Aquarium by Aliki
Swimmy by Leo Lionni
The Underwater Alphabet Book by Jerry Pallotta

More Underwater and *U* Activities

- Each day, hide a different underwater surprise in your water table. Try keys, coins, spoons, or colorful paper clips. Invite children to find, count, and sort their underwater treasures.

- Make some unique underwater art! Collect a clean baby food jar for each child. Have the child fill the jar with blue-tinted water and then sprinkle in her choice of sequins, bits of Mylar® wrapping, and plastic or metallic confetti.

- Play an underwater memory game. Draw waves on a section of your chalkboard to represent water. Cut out several construction paper fish, each a different color. Attach a strip of magnetic tape to the back of each fish. Display the fish on the board and ask youngsters to study the underwater scene for a minute. Then have them close their eyes. Remove one of the fish; then ask which fish is missing. Who can remember?

- Add an appliance box submarine to your dramatic play area so your youngsters can go on some underwater adventures. Simply cut some round portholes in the sides of the box and add a paper propeller to the back. Provide swimming goggles and fins in this center, too!

- Give each child a thin paper plate and ask her to imagine it's a submarine porthole. What does she see when she looks out? Have her draw an underwater scene in the center of the plate. Then staple a circle of blue cellophane or plastic wrap over the center to give her picture an underwater look.

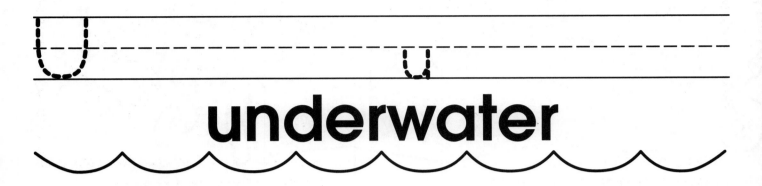

underwater

I am underwater.

I see...

What Is Underwater?

Name _____

A fish is underwater.

1

A shell is underwater.

2

©2001 The Education Center, Inc. • *Letter of the Week—Book 2* • TEC603

A plant is underwater.

3

I am underwater!

4

Shape Patterns
Use with *Sea Shapes* on page 145.

V Is for Village

Venture into this village of learning activities for the letter V.

Definition, Please?

As you begin studying villages and the letter *V,* ask your youngsters what they think a village is. As a class, decide on a definition and write it on a hut-shaped cutout. (If desired, work from the definition provided in the illustration.)

Village
A small group or community of homes

It Takes a Village

By Jane Cowen-Fletcher

This heartwarming tale shows the shared responsibility of a close-knit African community. Based on the African proverb "It takes a village to raise a child," this story shows just how that can happen! After reading and discussing this story, provide a doll or stuffed toy to serve as your class "child." Explain that this child can never be more than an arm's length away from a caretaker. Then begin by giving the doll to a chosen student. Over the next few days, encourage the whole class to pitch in to take care of the special child.

More Books About Villages

Appelemando's Dreams by Patricia Polacco
Daisy Rabbit's Tree House by Penny Dale
Ogbo: Sharing Life in an African Village by Ifeoma Onyefulu
Stone Soup by Marcia Brown
A Village Full of Valentines by James Stevenson

Village Puppets

Use these village puppets to help your youngsters discover some of the jobs that are necessary to keep a village running smoothly. Duplicate the people patterns on page 153 onto tagboard to make a class supply. Provide an assortment of construction paper, large craft sticks, and a variety of other art supplies. Working with one small group at a time, have each child cut out his person pattern. Then facilitate a discussion about what kinds of jobs are necessary in a village. Encourage each child to use the art supplies to decorate his pattern to resemble the village worker of his choice. Then have him glue a craft stick handle to the back of his puppet. Later, invite children to use their puppets as props when they sing "Village Workers" (see below).

Village Workers

Sing this song to the tune of "London Bridge." Encourage students to add new verses, substituting different kinds of village workers. Have each child hold up his puppet as appropriate.

The village baker bakes the bread,
Bakes the bread, bakes the bread.
The village baker bakes the bread,
Village baker.

Additional ideas:
*butcher, cuts the meat
tailor, sews the clothes
peddler, sells his wares
cobbler, makes our shoes
weaver, weaves a basket
doctor, makes us well
postmaster, gives us mail
innkeeper, rents a room*

The Village of *V*

There's a variety of *V* words behind the doors of this creative letter-reinforcing activity. In advance, copy pages 154–156 on brown construction paper for each child. Have each child cut out the door patterns and then glue each door onto a different hut. Next, have her glue both sets of huts together at the ends so that they'll stand to make a little circular village. Encourage students to read the *V* words behind each door.

Village Vegetable Soup

The village for this activity is your classroom, and the vegetables are a hodgepodge of what your little villagers bring! Ask each child to bring a vegetable to school on a given day. In the morning, help each child wash and chop her vegetable. Then ask her to put her vegetable in a slow cooker. When all the vegetables are in the pot, add chicken broth to the pot until it is a couple of inches from the top. Set the cooker on low and let the village vegetable soup simmer until the veggies are soft.

Village Book Page

There's a very big vine in the village! And just what grows on it is up to your students' imaginations! Use the *V* book page on page 157 as directed for the letter *A*. Have each child write or dictate to complete the story starter and then color and illustrate the page.

More Village and *V* Activities

- Host a village variety show! Invite each child to prepare a special act for the class, such as reciting a poem, singing a song, or performing a dance. On the day of the variety show, sit back and soak it up!

- Encourage children to make their own village in your block area. To make a village house, stuff a brown paper lunch bag three-fourths full with crumpled newspaper. Fold and staple the top portion down. Use a black marker to draw windows and a door. Then glue raffia strips to the roof. Invite children to arrange their houses in your block area to create their own unique village.

People Patterns

Use with "Village Puppets" and "Village Workers" on page 151.

Village Hut Patterns
Use with "The Village of *V*" on page 152.

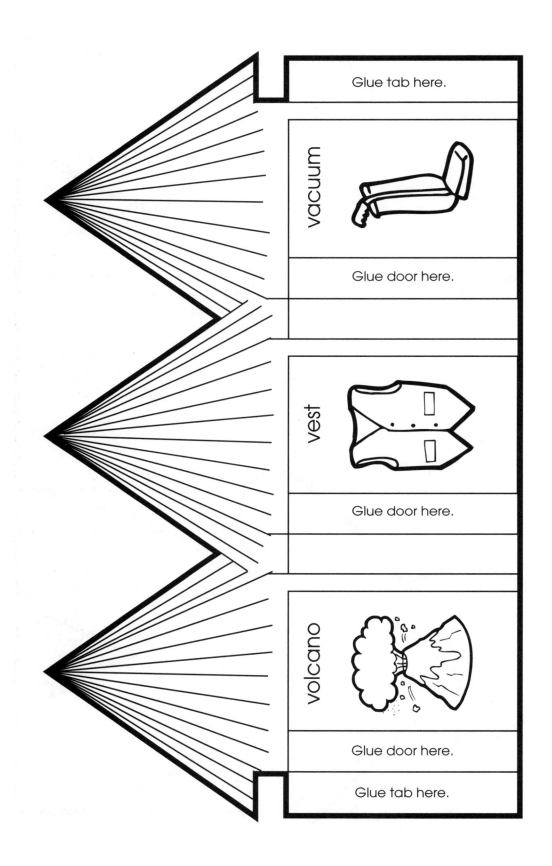

Glue tab here.

vacuum

Glue door here.

vest

Glue door here.

volcano

Glue door here.

Glue tab here.

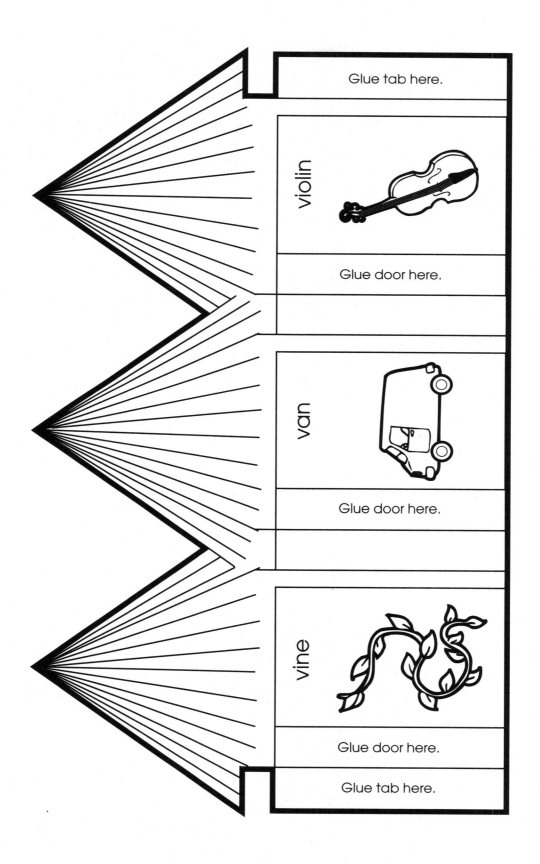

Glue tab here.

violin

Glue door here.

van

Glue door here.

vine

Glue door here.

Glue tab here.

Door Patterns
Use with "The Village of *V*" on page 152.

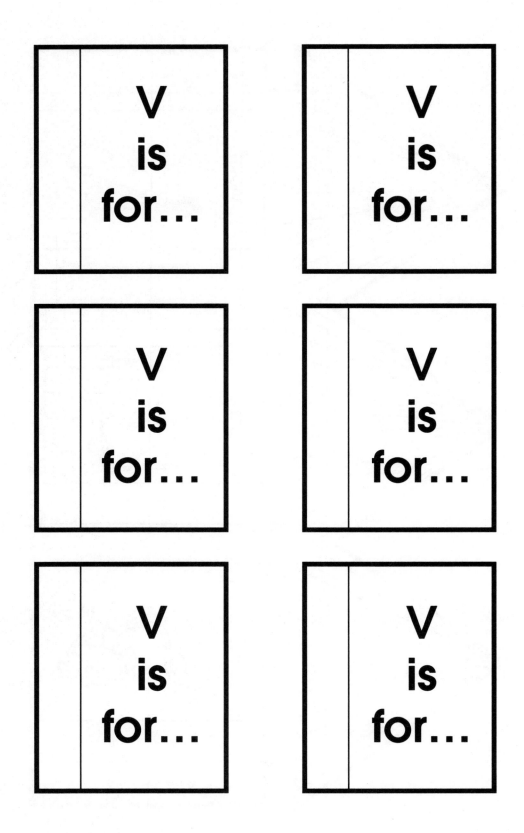

village

There is a very big vine in the village!

It grows...

W Is for Walrus

Learn about the letter W with these wonderful walrus ideas.

Waddle Like a Walrus

Encourage youngsters to work up some actions to go along with this walrus rhyme.

Waddle Like a Walrus
Waddle like a walrus,
Step, two, three.
Show your tusks,
As long as can be.
Wiggle your whiskers.
Flap your flippers.
Then ready, set, dive
Into the deep blue sea!

Walrus Cookies

Set out the supplies listed below; then invite each child to assemble his own edible walrus!

Ingredients for one:
large sugar cookie
vanilla wafer (broken in half)
gumdrop nose
M&M's® candy eyes
banana tusks (sliced lengthwise)
peanut butter glue

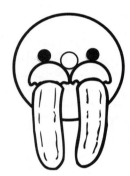

Walrus Puppet Pal

Reinforce *W* words with this three-dimensional puppet. For each child, copy the walrus patterns on pages 161–162 on white construction paper. To make the puppet, color and cut out the patterns. Then cut slits on the head where indicated. Glue the tusks on the nose section. Next, glue the straight edges in the middle of the nose section together, forming the snout shape. Insert the nose tabs into the slits on the head and tape the tabs in place on the back of the head. To make a handle, glue a large craft stick to the back of the puppet. Invite each child to walk her walrus pal around the room to "read" *W* words. Or have her create walrus dialogue and stories with her fellow walruses.

Walrus Book Page

Use the *W* book page on page 160 as directed for the letter *A*. How does Mr. Walrus stay warm in the winter? Ask each child to color her page and write or dictate how she thinks her walrus stays warm in the winter. Answers can be factual or fanciful. Perhaps your walrus will wear a *wig!*

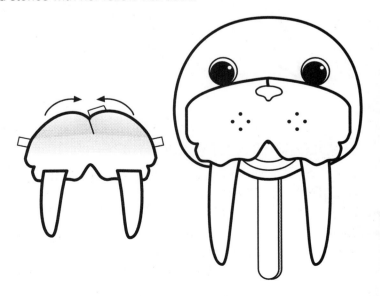

What's in the Window, Walrus?

What wonders does Walrus see through his window? Invite each child to make this igloo to share in Walrus's view. Have each child color and cut out a copy of the igloo and window patterns (pages 163–164). Then have her stack all the pictures, adding the titled window on top. Help her staple the stack onto the igloo where indicated. Encourage children to read their books aloud together.

Little Walrus Warning
By Carol Young

While learning to become independent, Little Walrus saves his herd from approaching danger! After sharing this story, invite your youngsters to play this musical iceberg game. Cut out ten large icebergs from white bulletin board paper. Label each one with a different numeral from 1 to 10 and laminate them. Then label a set of notecards from 1 to 10 and place them in a bag. Randomly arrange the icebergs on the floor. Choose a student to be the caller and assign each remaining student the role of a walrus. To play, the walruses "swim" around the icebergs to a selection of lively music. When the music stops, each walrus moves onto an iceberg. The caller draws a card from the bag and reads the numeral aloud. The walruses on the iceberg with the matching number are "tipped" over into the sea. The tipped iceberg is removed from the sea and play continues until one iceberg remains. How many walruses survived the tipping icebergs?

Wonderful Walrus Reads

Walrus (Nature's Children series) by Laima Dingwall
The Walrus and the Carpenter by Lewis Carroll

More Walrus and *W* Activities

- On several sentence strips, write alliterative sentences that contain lots of *W* words. Then invite each child to illustrate his choice of sentences. As each child shares his illustration, have him show the corresponding sentence strip. As a class, read/recite the sentences together.

- Ask each child to draw a walrus making a wish; then write her dictation on a speech bubble cutout. Have the child glue her speech bubble to her drawing. Later, invite her to share her walrus's wish with the class.

- Give each child a yarn worm for this wiggly word game. Walk around your classroom with a pointer, randomly touching words displayed in the classroom. If the word begins with *W,* all the children wiggle their worms in the air.

W   w

walrus

How does Mr. Walrus stay warm in the winter?

He...

head

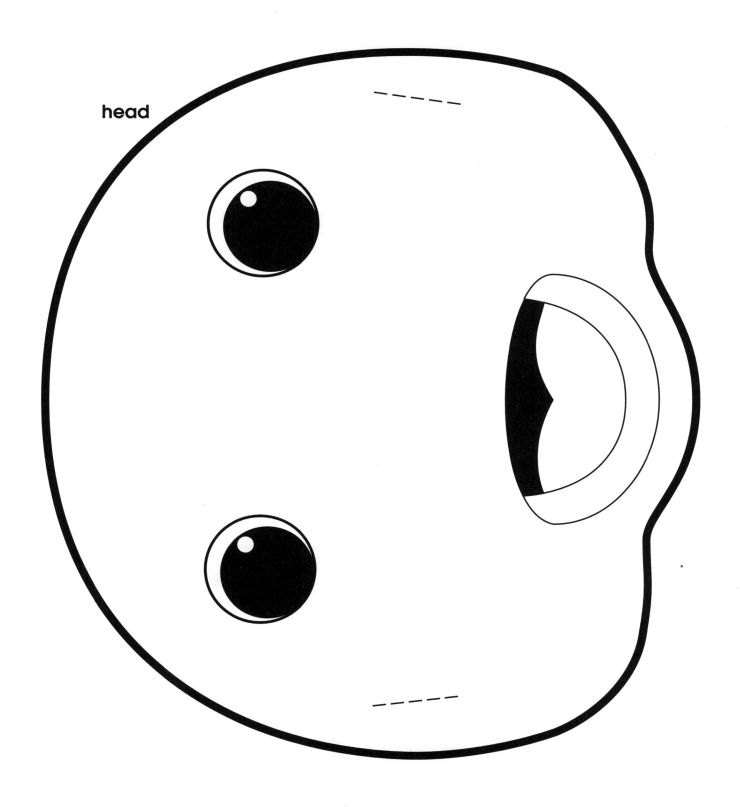

Walrus Patterns
Use with "Walrus Puppet Pal" on page 158.

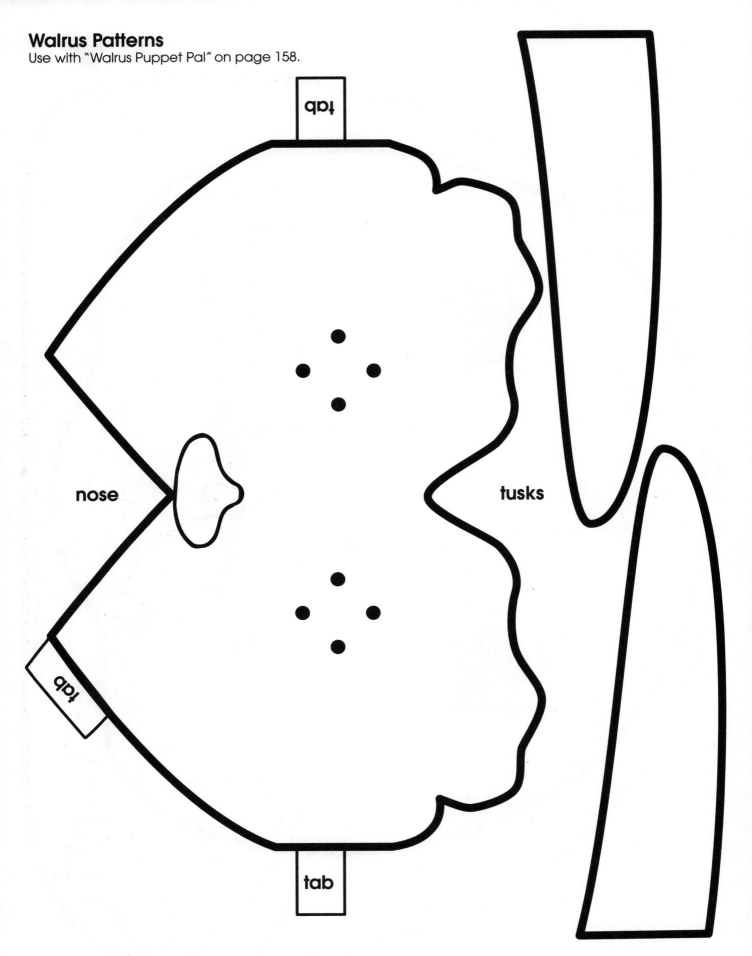

nose

tusks

tab

tab

tab

Staple here.

Staple here.

Window Patterns
Use with "What's in the Window, Walrus?" on page 159.

What's in the Window, Walrus?

wagon

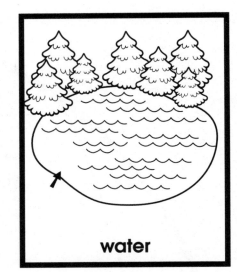
water

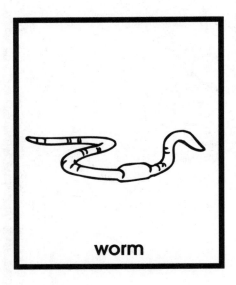
worm

web

watch

watermelon

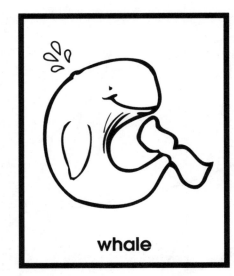
whale

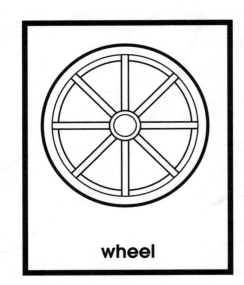
wheel

X Is for EXtra Special

Your students will learn about each other and study the letter X at the same time!

Extra Special Me!

Sing this song to the tune of "Bingo." When you spell *extra* and you get to the *X*, have each child make an *X* in the air with her arms. After the song, invite each child to share something special about herself.

Extra Special Me
There are some things
That make me me
And really like no other.
E-**X**-T-R-A, E-**X**-T-R-A, E-**X**-T-R-A,
I'm extra special me!

Extra Special Countdown

Use this little rhyme to practice counting backward. Encourage each child to make up actions to go along with the words and to use his fingers to show the corresponding number.

Extra Special Countdown
Five extra special fingers
That help me work all day.

Four extra special friends
That help me laugh and play.

Three extra special words
For saying "I love you."

Two extra special people—
That must be me and you!

One extra special me;
I'm all that's left, you see.

'Cause I'm the only one of me;
I'm extra special me!

Edible *X*

Mmmm, edible *X*s—no two are exactly alike! Have children lightly flour their hands to prepare for this activity. Then give each child a portion of cold sugar cookie dough. Instruct him to roll out two dough snakes. Then have him arrange the two snakes to form an *X*. Encourage each child to use various cake decorations and sprinkles to decorate his *X*. Then bake the cookies according to the recipe directions.

Extra Special Book Page

Use the *X* book page on page 167 as directed for the letter *A*. Ask each child to write or dictate to complete the sentence starter. Then invite him to color and decorate the person to resemble himself.

My Extra Special *X* Book

These child-made booklets will help reinforce that tricky letter *X*. In advance, photocopy pages 168–171 for each child. Have each child cut apart her booklet pages and cover, sequence them, and staple them along the left edge. Then have her personalize her cover. Read each booklet page together; then have each child find and cut out the picture that matches that sentence. Instruct her to glue the picture to the page and then decorate the page with colorful *X*s. During a group time, read the books together.

X O X O

Send kisses and hugs all around! First, discuss how *X*s and *O*s are often used to represent kisses and hugs. Then provide sponges cut in *X* and *O* shapes and different colors of paint. Give each child a sheet of art paper and encourage him to print a pattern to give to an extra special person in his life.

More Extra Special Books

Chrysanthemum by Kevin Henkes
Eggbert: The Slightly Cracked Egg by Tom Ross
An Extraordinary Egg by Leo Lionni
Isaac the Ice Cream Truck by Scott Santoro

ABC I Like Me
By Nancy Carlson

Nancy Carlson's cheerful pig brings along a few friends to reinforce the alphabet as well as the joy of happy thoughts about oneself. After sharing this book, title a display "ABC, I Like Me!" Ask each child to think of something that he likes about himself. Then have him write his name on a sentence strip, followed by his chosen characteristic. Post each child's strip under the titled display. Invite each child to draw an illustration to go with his writing.

More Extra Special and *X* Activities

- Try this extra special art idea. Fold a sheet of colorful construction paper in half. Make snips and cuts on each side of the folded paper without going completely through to one side or the other (see the illustration). Then open up the paper to reveal one side that looks exactly like the other! Back the artwork with another colorful piece of construction paper.

- During your study of *X,* provide some real X rays for your science center! Ask local hospitals or labs to donate old or imperfect X-ray films. Show children how to put an X ray up to a window or lighted area to examine it. Can you guess what it is? How can you tell?

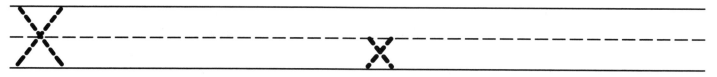

extra special

I am extra special because…

1

X is in exercise.

My Extra Special X Book

by _____

3

X is in fox.

2

X is in X ray.

Booklet Pages

Use with "My Extra Special *X* Book" on page 166.

5

X is in exit.

4

X is in ax.

exercise

X ray

fox

ax

exit

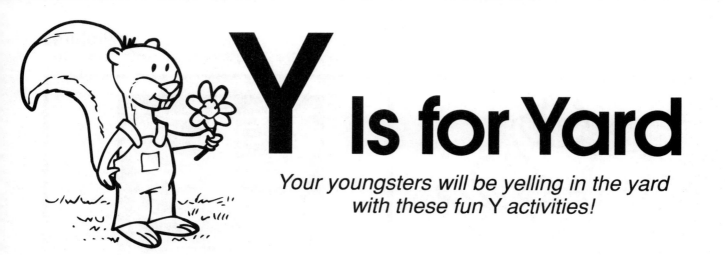

Y Is for Yard

Your youngsters will be yelling in the yard with these fun Y activities!

Yelling in the Yard

Introduce your little ones to the letter *Y* with this lively yelling rhyme. Of course, you might want to take them outdoors for this lesson!

I'm yelling in the yard,
A sound you cannot miss.
For when I [am a cowboy],
I yell like this:
"[Yee-haw]!"

Each time you repeat the rhyme, replace the underlined words with one of the following sets of phrases. Or make up your own phrases to fit the rhyme.

call my friends, "Yoo-hoo!"
shout for joy, "Yippee!"
yodel a song, "Yodel-ay-hee-hoo!"

Yard Book Page

Use the *Y* book page on page 174 as directed for the letter *A*. Give each child a copy of page 174 and a yellow crayon. Then ask her to fill her yard with yellow things, such as a ball, a bird, a bicycle, and a patch of flowers. Have her write or dictate to complete the story starter in the space provided. Then invite her to finish coloring her yard scene with a variety of other colors.

Y Tree Art

After your students create these interesting trees, they just might discover some similar-looking trees in nearby yards! To begin, ask each child to use a pencil to draw a giant *Y* on a sheet of art paper. Then have him add Y-shaped branches to the tree. Next, ask the child to paint over the pencil lines with brown paint. After the paint dries, have him sponge-paint little leaves on the branches.

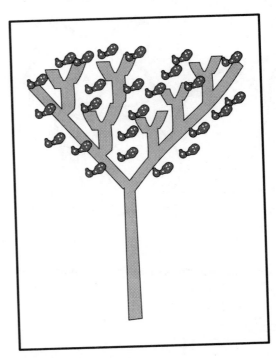

Yummy Yams

Where are yams grown? In someone's *yard,* of course! Enlist the help of your youngsters to mix up their own individual servings of this yummy yam treat. For every three to four children, heat a can of cut yams. Let the yams cool a little; then drain them. Give each child a small serving on a plastic plate. Have the child mash his yams with a fork. Then have him stir in a pat of butter and eight mini marshmallows. Yum!

My Spring Robin
By Anne Rockwell

When spring arrives, a young girl searches her yard to find her spring robin. After reading the story, challenge students' visual skills with this foldout booklet. For each child, copy the booklet pages on pages 176–177 and—according to his ability level—the word or picture wheel on page 178. Have each child cut out and glue his pages together where indicated. Ask him to color the yard scene and, if applicable, his picture wheel. Then help him cut out the dotted-line opening on the first page, attach his wheel with a paper fastener, and accordion-fold his booklet. To use, the child turns the wheel to reveal a word or picture. Then he finds the corresponding picture in the scene.

Yippee for Yard Books!
Jack's Garden by Henry Cole
Ten Flashing Fireflies by Philemon Sturges

Yellow Yo-Yo

The yard is the perfect place to master new yo-yo tricks. And this special yo-yo will help youngsters master those tricky *Y* words. For each child, copy the yo-yo patterns on page 175 onto yellow paper. Also copy the word circles on page 178 onto white paper. Ask each child to cut out all of her patterns. Have her glue each word circle where indicated over the corresponding picture. Then help her tie one end of a length of yellow yarn into a loop. To assemble the yo-yo, have the child staple the cover to the back, trapping the loose end of the yarn between the pages. Encourage each child to read each word inside her yo-yo and then lift the flap to self-check.

More Yard and *Y* Activities

- Shine a projector toward a blank wall and dim the lights. Invite small groups of children to experiment with using their bodies to make shadows. Then encourage each child to make a *Y* on the wall.

- Divide a sheet of bulletin board paper into two columns. Label one column "Yuck" and the other "Yum." Add a corresponding frowning and smiley face, if desired. Then ask each child to draw or glue a food picture in each column to indicate his feeling about the food. Later, invite students to tell the class about their pictures and preferences.

- Create a winding, looping path on the floor with yellow tape. Or draw a path with yellow sidewalk chalk on an outdoor paved surface. Invite students to follow the yellow brick road in a variety of ways, such as jumping, skipping, or walking on tiptoe.

yard

My yard has many yellow things.

I see...

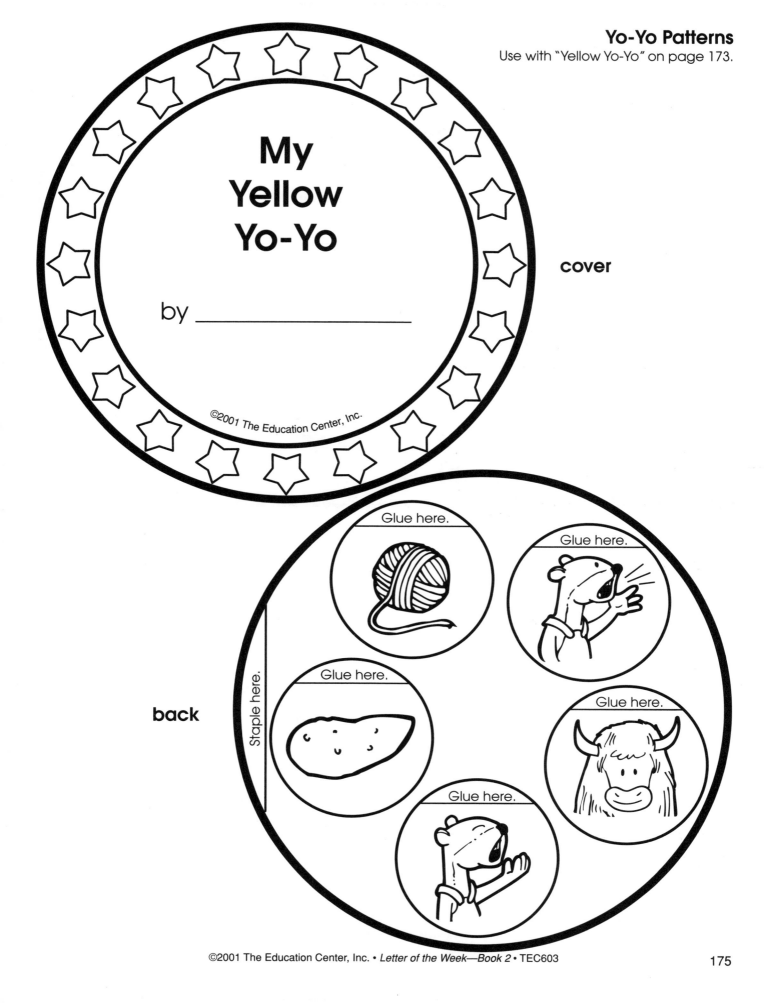

My Yellow Yo-Yo

by _____

cover

©2001 The Education Center, Inc.

back

Glue here.

Glue here.

Staple here.

Glue here.

Glue here.

Glue here.

In the Yard

by

©The Education Center, Inc.

Cut out.

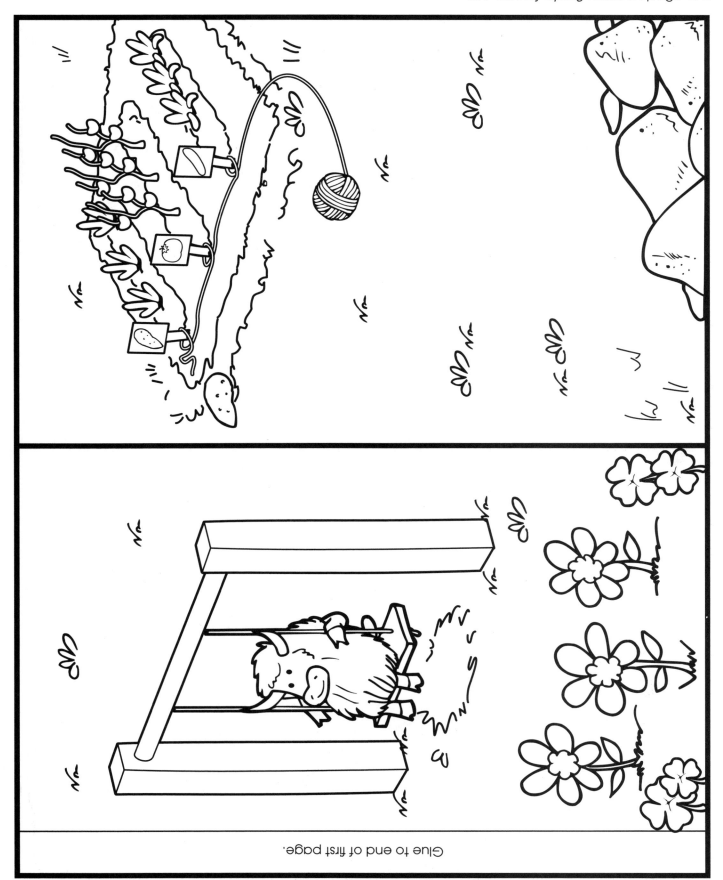

Glue to end of first page.

Word Wheel and Picture Wheel Patterns

Use with *My Spring Robin* on page 173.

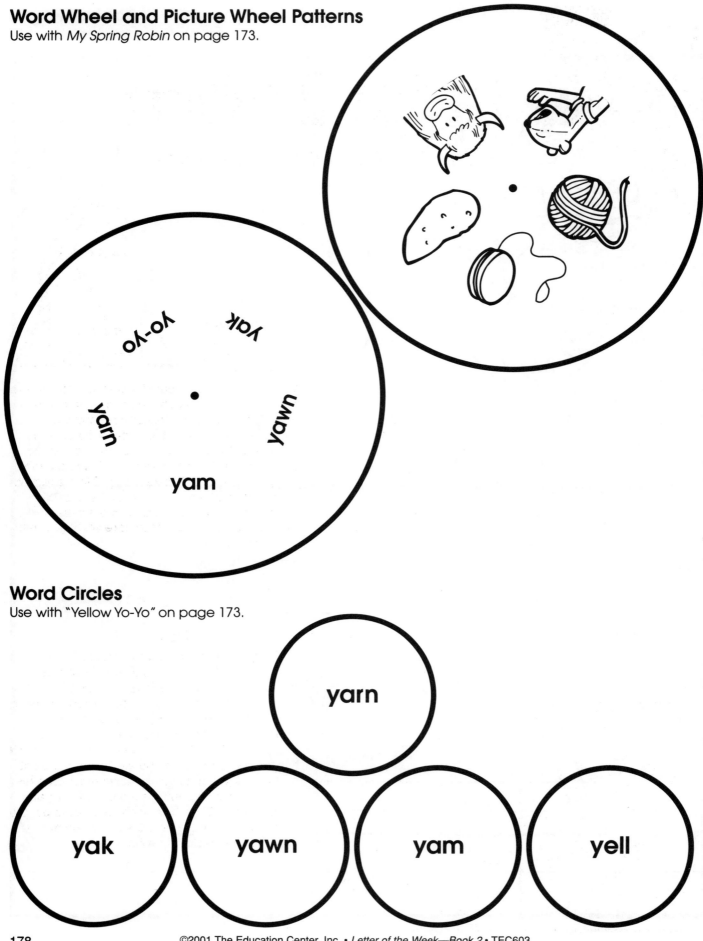

Word Circles

Use with "Yellow Yo-Yo" on page 173.

yarn

yak   yawn   yam   yell

©2001 The Education Center, Inc. • *Letter of the Week—Book 2* • TEC603

Z Is for Zoom

Zoom in on the letter Z with these zippy ideas!

Zippy Little Melody

Get your youngsters moving to this zesty little song sung to the tune of "Zip-a-dee-doo-dah."

Zip-a-dee-doo-dah, zip-a-dee-ay,
I like to zoom-zoom around all day!
I am a(n) [race car] zooming this way.
Zip-a-dee-doo-dah, zip-a-dee-ay!

Each time you repeat the song, replace the underlined word with a word or phrase for a fast-moving item, such as *airplane, freight train, speedboat, rocket, skateboard, ostrich,* or *cheetah.*

Rocket Delights

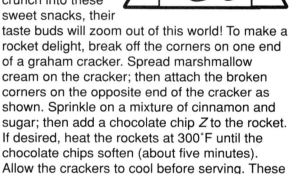

When students crunch into these sweet snacks, their taste buds will zoom out of this world! To make a rocket delight, break off the corners on one end of a graham cracker. Spread marshmallow cream on the cracker; then attach the broken corners on the opposite end of the cracker as shown. Sprinkle on a mixture of cinnamon and sugar; then add a chocolate chip *Z* to the rocket. If desired, heat the rockets at 300°F until the chocolate chips soften (about five minutes). Allow the crackers to cool before serving. These treats will go fast!

Zip-It Art

Zoom into this zany art technique! Provide each child with a gallon-size resealable plastic bag and a 10½" square of white paper. Have the child slide the paper into the bag. Then have him dip a few cotton balls and cotton swabs into different paint colors and drop them into the bag. Help the child zip his bag; then have him shake it so that the cotton balls and swabs spread paint all over his paper. When he finishes creating his zany art, have him remove the cotton balls and cotton swabs. Then help each child press out the air and zip the bag again. Display these masterpieces with the title "Zip-It Art."

I like to go zooming around in a... rocket ship.

Zoom Book Page

How do your students like to zoom around? Use the *Z* book page on page 181 as directed for the letter *A.* Discuss students' vehicle choices; then have each child draw her preference on a copy of page 181. Have her write or dictate to complete the story starter in the space provided.

x

Zip! Zoom! Zing!

A buzzing little bee zips, zooms, and zings all around this zoo booklet. For each child, copy pages 182–184 and the bee pattern on page 185. Cut slits along the dotted lines on each booklet cover. Have each child color and cut out her booklet cover, booklet pages, and bee. Then have her cut along the dotted lines on booklet page 1. Have each child stack her pages in order and staple them together along the left side. To make the manipulative bee, glue the bee cutout to a mini craft stick; then insert the stick through the slits in the cover. Encourage each child to remove the bee and manipulate it through the zoo according to the text. Bzzz!

Zoom Away With These Books

Cosmo Zooms by Arthur Howard
Mama Zooms by Jane Cowen-Fletcher
Zoom, Zoom, Fire Engine! by Iain Smyth

What's Faster Than a Speeding Cheetah?
By Robert E. Wells

Share this book about speedy things; then invite your students to make these puzzles featuring things that zoom. To prepare, make a tagboard copy of the picture on page 185 for each child. Have each child color his picture and then cut it out along the bold outline. Instruct him to puzzle-cut the picture into several pieces. Then have him store his puzzle pieces in a zippered plastic bag. Invite each child to assemble his own or a classmate's puzzle. How fast can he put it together?

More Zoom and *Z* Activities

- Zip up a jacket or sweater and turn it inside out. Then slip a piece of sturdy cardboard inside. Invite each child to cover the zipper with a piece of paper and experiment rubbing over it with the sides of crayons. Can she make a zipper *Z*?

- To make a zoomer, ask each child to color a toilet paper tube. Then have him cut out construction paper wings. Help him tape a piece of waxed paper over one end of the tube and then tape the wings to the tube. Then invite him to hold the open end of the tube to his mouth and "zoom" around the room.

- Ask each child to cut out zigzag strips of assorted paper products. Then invite her to use the strips to create a colorful zigzag collage.

zoom

I like to go zooming around in a...

Zip! Zoom! Zing!

by _____

Zip into the zoo.

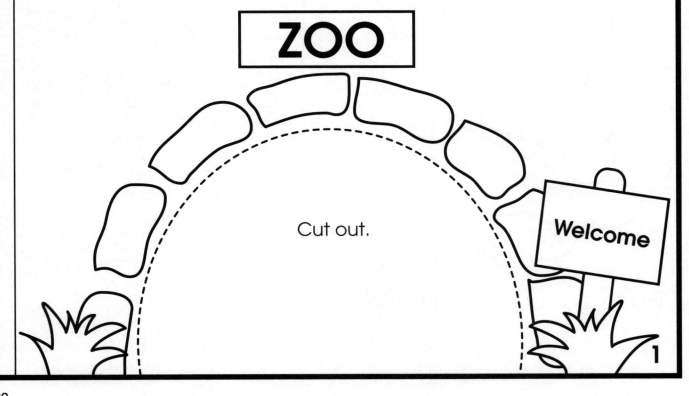

ZOO

Cut out.

Welcome

1

Zoom through the Zs!

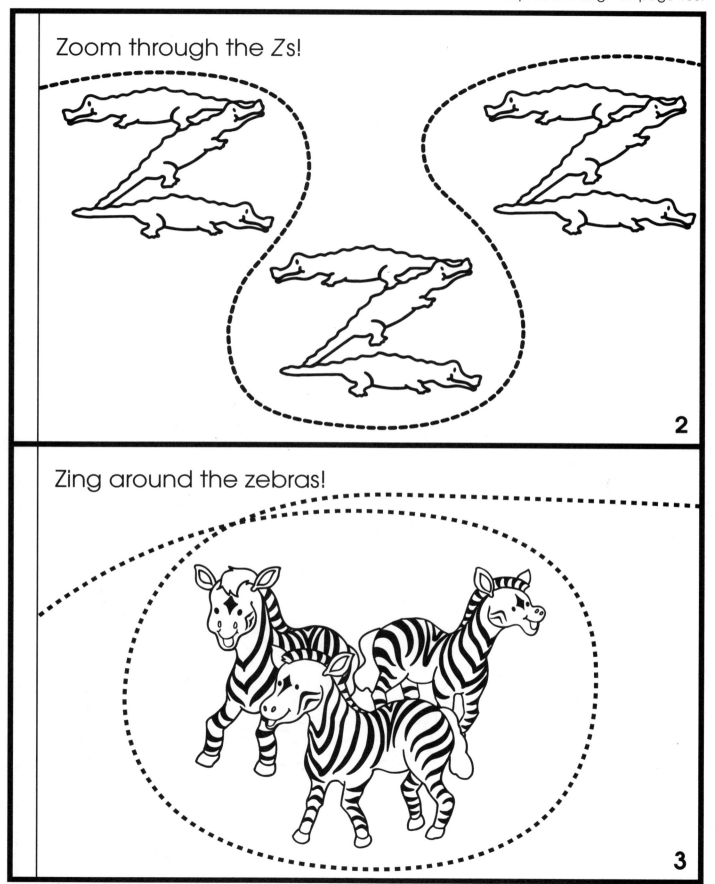

2

Zing around the zebras!

3

Zip under the zeros.

4

Zoom over the Zinnias!

5

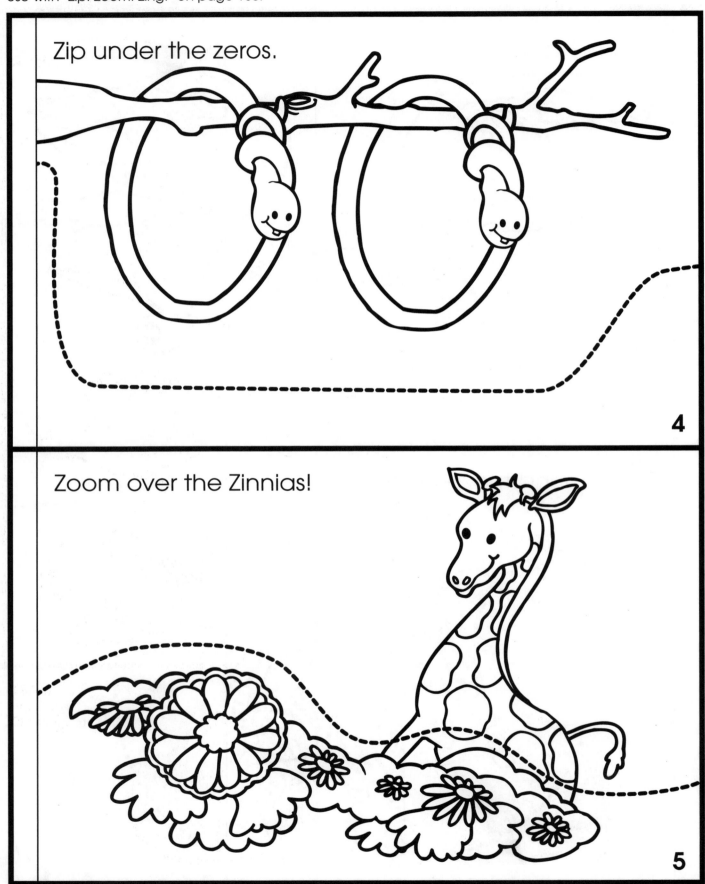

Puzzle Pattern

Use with *What's Faster Than a Speeding Cheetah?* on page 180.

Bees

Use with "Zip! Zoom! Zing!" on page 180.

Additional Alphabet Books

- *A My Name Is...* by Alice Lyne
- *The A to Z Beastly Jamboree* by Robert Bender
- *ABC Animal Riddles* by Susan Joyce
- *ABC Book* by C. B. Falls
- *ABC Discovery!* by Izhar Cohen
- *ABC Pop!* by Rachel Isadora
- *Alphabet City* by Stephen T. Johnson
- *Alpha Bugs* by David A. Carter
- *Amazing Animal Alphabet* by Richard Edwards
- *An Alphabet of Dinosaurs* by Peter Dodson
- *Animalia* by Graeme Base
- *Arches to Zigzags: An Architecture ABC* by Michael J. Crosbie
- *From Anne to Zach* by Mary Jane Martin
- *A Gardener's Alphabet* by Mary Azarian
- *Handsigns: A Sign Language Alphabet* by Kathleen Fain
- *The Hullabaloo ABC* by Beverly Cleary
- *The Letters Are Lost!* by Lisa Campbell Ernst

Award

Congratulations!

_____
student's name

has worked hard to
learn all the letters
of the alphabet and
their sounds.

_____
date

_____
teacher's name

My Alphabet Book

by
_____

- - - - - - - - - - - - - - - - - - -

_____